THE SHABBY PARADISE

EILEEN BAILLIE

The Shabby Paradise

The Autobiography of a Decade

DECORATIONS BY

DICK HART

HUTCHINSON OF LONDON

HUTCHINSON & CO. *(Publishers)* LTD
178–202 *Great Portland Street, London, W.*1

London Melbourne Sydney
Auckland Bombay Toronto
Johannesburg New York

★

First Published July 1958
Second Impression July 1958
Third Impression September 1958

© Eileen Baillie 1958

Set in eleven on thirteen point Bell
and printed in Great Britain by
Tonbridge Printers Ltd,
Tonbridge, Kent

TO

My Mother and the Memory
of my Father

CONTENTS

FOREWORD

No less a person than Joseph Conrad once commented upon the close and apparently natural connection between the church and the sea. It is borne out yet once again in this story of a childhood spent in the dockland parish of which my father was the vicar.

My family left the London River, but I came back to it; for if I failed to achieve my first childish ambition to become a sailor and spend my life at sea, I attained the second. I married, if not a sea-captain, a seafaring man who became, later in his career, the master of some very fine ships and ultimately Commodore of one of those great shipping companies about which I used to sing, with impartial fervour, from the pages of the *Just So Song Book*, in those early years.

1. View from a Slum Window

ALTHOUGH I had been born, at the beginning of the century, into the irreproachable environment of an elegant Bayswater terrace, I was to grow up, by violent contrast, in the dubious surroundings of a slum; for soon after my first birthday my parents moved to a Dockland parish in the East End of London, where I was to spend the early and more impressionable years of childhood.

From the curacy of a fashionable West End church such as Christ Church, Lancaster Gate, to the incumbency of St Michael-and-All-Angels, Bromley-by-Bow, Poplar, is a far cry in everything save actual distance. Possibly my father was already beginning to find the superficial routine of a prosperous parish irksome. He was not the kind of man to tolerate with ease the crowded, wealthy congregations who came, quite simply, to criticise each other's clothes and the preacher's sermons; nor the scale of values that obliged a stranger to remain standing in the porch until the bell had stopped ringing for fear that he might unwittingly displace a late arrival who had paid rent for his pew. (To the end of his ministry my

11

father waged an unremitting war on pew-rents.) And the young couple must have grown weary of the spate of social engagements with which they were inundated. During the Season, the piles of thick, white invitation cards grew embarrassingly high on the drawing-room mantelpiece of the tall, narrow house in Devonshire Terrace. The curate and his wife were eminently presentable, and they were popular; they could have filled their engagement-book two or three times over with functions that could not, by any stretch of the imagination, be described as parochial. For Lancaster Gate, as the nineteenth century merged into the twentieth, was still a fashionable residential district of private houses owned and occupied by the well-to-do, overshadowed by no hint of its coming change of fortune into a dreary desert of hotels and boarding-houses largely inhabited by the rootless, the penurious, and the pensioned.

Fifty years ago, Poplar was considered by those who did not have to live there to be a fearsome part of the world, with a rough and dangerous population consisting in the main of criminals, drunkards, and even anarchists: a place prone to virulent epidemics, a cradle of industrial unrest, a haunt of vice and vermin. To my father it offered the chance and the challenge he desired. He grasped his opportunity with all the exuberance of an energetic nature and the enthusiasm of a man in the prime of his vigour. He was but thirty-five when, towards the end of the year 1904, he was inducted into the living, and brought my mother, my elder sister and myself from the aristocratic purlieus of Hyde Park to the dingy Vicarage at the top of a narrow turning off the East India Dock Road.

People were horrified at the idea of taking small children to live in such surroundings. A child of six, and a baby just over one year old! Well-meaning relatives begged my father to reconsider his rash decision before it was too late—'for the children's sake, if not for Katie's!'—Katie, of course, being my mother. How wise he was not to listen to them! It proved to be the happiest decade of his life.

The Docks of what is still the greatest port in the world lie eastwards and down-river from the Tower to Tilbury, strung out at ever-widening intervals along the twisting course of the Thames: only twenty miles of it in all, and yet, in terms of history, commerce, shipping, and the lives of men, as closely packed a stretch as any twenty miles in Christendom.

Beginning on the northern shore with the small, enclosed basins of St Katharine's, their waters dark and still between the cliff-like walls of warehouses, through the growing range of the London Docks, the West India—giant marvel of the nineteenth century's opening years—and the East India Docks, they develop into the vast acreage of the Royal Group, where a whole settlement of ships rises against the sky-line to dwarf the grovelling houses of East Ham and Silvertown. They end at Tilbury, where the largest ships ever to round the North Foreland lie berthed in strange proximity to a waste of reed-beds and low scrub, infested with rabbits, rats, and cats, and the haunt in May and June of nightingales.

Tilbury, however, is scarcely to be regarded as included within the confines of authentic Dockland. It is too remote, too cut off by long reaches of bleak Essex marsh, beyond which the vessels passing up and down the Thames appear to ride high above the land. Besides, Tilbury is still a countrified spot, with clean, strong winds blowing in from the North Sea, larks singing over the marsh pastures, and cattle feeding on the coarse, juicy grasses of the estuarial plain.

Dockland proper, where people lead their lives, hard and rough maybe, but none the less varied, at close quarters in a maze of noisy streets crowded with traffic, against an eternal background of crane-jibs, the funnels of ships and warehouse walls, can be narrowed to an area with geographical boundaries as sharply defined as its local colour and characteristics. You will find it 'east of Aldgate Pump' and westward of Barking; and you need go no further north than the White-chapel High Street. Turn off down the Commercial Road, where the foreign names on the fascia-boards of shops are two to every one in English and the printed matter displayed on hoardings is frequently in Yiddish; keep on to the junction of East India Dock Road and West India Dock Road, where the Yiddish gives place to Chinese characters, and the kosher shop to the Chop Suey eating-house; then, having traversed the parishes of Whitechapel, Shadwell and Limehouse—all sub-divisions of the ancient parish of Stepney—you will come to Poplar, bordered on the east by the River Lea, on the north and west by the Limehouse Cut, and to the south by that strange elbow of land held in a deep crook of the Thames and known as the Isle of Dogs.

Even today it is a poor district, a shabby district. There are few fine buildings and a multitude of squalid ones, although the neat yellow brick cubes of Lansbury are a model of what a city housing estate should be. The streets are monotonous, the outlook dreary, the atmosphere tainted with the stench of factories and damp with the breath of nearby Thames. You are in East London, a name which, half a century ago, was still synonymous with the extremes of poverty, crime, hunger, disease and dirt: in plain language, a slum. And Poplar was a bad slum; it might be said to have achieved pride of place at the bottom of the scale of slums, though many would have given that dubious palm to Bermondsey across the River. But Bermondsey notwithstanding, Poplar could hold its own with its neighbours to the north and west, Bethnal Green, Hoxton, Limehouse and Wapping, in notoriety for the grievous conditions, both physical and spiritual, in which its inhabitants were obliged to exist.

Nowadays it is modish to profess an agreeable nostalgia for the past; there is a vogue for reminiscence, for wistful evocations of one's earliest childhood memories. Such descriptions of beautiful old houses, mellow walled gardens full of forbidden fruits, of favourite trout-streams and familiar fields, only serve to make me conscious of the abyss that separates me from these delicate chronicles.

Of what different substance was my 'lost paradise of youth': a shabby street of squalid houses and shops, unrelieved by tree or shrub, punctuated by nothing more notable than the crude decorations and false gaiety of the public-house. Thus you will find St Leonard's Road today, running northwards from the East India Dock Road where it widens opposite the entrance to the Blackwall Tunnel and the unexpectedly imposing entrance to the Docks; and at its top, the Church and Vicarage of blackened brick, built on a triangle of land that is the meeting-place of many streets. Church and house stood side by side—still stand, indeed, unscathed by the bombing of two wars and in externals exactly as I knew them half a century ago—in a fringe of sooty London plane-trees, an oasis not only of foliage but of devotion in that deadly pattern of dreary pavements and drab house-fronts.

Neither building could ever have been handsome. In the first half of the nineteenth century the rapid growth of London's eastern suburbs, running like rank weeds into the country fields under the pressure of the industrial revolution and the feverish development of seaborne trade, alarmed their Spiritual Lordships into the hurried erection of many such churches which had little to recommend them architecturally. St Michael's, built in the 'sixties, could be dismissed in two words as Victorian-utilitarian. Constructed of grimy brick without and a good deal of splintery varnished pitch-pine within, it was at once conventional and singularly featureless, save for a tall tower finished off by a sort of cocked hat of slates, visible for miles around and to me, at any rate, a landmark of supreme importance. On each of its four sides the tower displayed a clock-face, illuminated at night; and in those days, before the invention of wireless telegraphy and the Greenwich Time Signal, I dare say the whole neighbourhood looked to it when they wanted to know the hour, for such clocks as they possessed spent much of their lives reposing in the pawnbroker's window.

Useful as our church-tower may have been to the parish, no one but myself could measure the exact extent of its significance in my own eyes. After dark I would look regularly for the round orange face through the landing window on my way to bed, or pick out its steady glow above the house-tops as we returned from some winter outing. Invariably it produced a feeling of indescribable comfort and reassurance. The moon might have omitted to complete her orbit, the sun have failed to rise—I should have been less perturbed than if the clock in St Michael's tower had remained unlit after the fall of darkness! To this day, I have only to catch a glimpse of that unmistakable, familiar outline, which can be seen from Canning Town Bridge and, in clear weather from the Fenchurch Street railway, to experience all over again a small, warm sensation of inner well-being: almost as though I had received a benediction.

Close alongside the Church squatted the Vicarage, huddling gratefully for shelter and protection beneath the shadow of its consecrated neighbour. It was even less inspiring. The front-door and all the windows were surmounted by ecclesiastical-looking pointed arches, possibly intended to induce a pious frame of mind in the beholder without as well as the dweller within. A hedge of struggling privet screened the ground-floor rooms; the plane-trees dripped poisonously on to the little garden which for most of the year contained little but sour earth and a smell of cats, in spite of my mother's spirited attempts at cultivation.

I have often wondered what sort of impression it could have made on her when she saw it for the first time, probably on a day in late autumn when the fog was rolling up from the river and the pavements were greasy with sooty rain. As the daughter, niece, and granddaughter of clergymen, in addition to being a woman of considerable moral courage and an unyielding sense of duty, she would have been no more than faintly daunted.

My sister was quite old enough to make invidious comparisons between Lancaster Gate and Poplar. From the lofty eminence of her five years' seniority she must have regarded the change in our surroundings with some dismay. No parks to play in, and for sole companion a baby sister! In those early months she must often have sighed for the children's tea-parties of Bayswater, the playmates of the Round Pond, and the green slopes of Kensington Gardens.

Of the whole family, I was the only one to have no memories. I had never known another home; yet as soon as I became conscious of my own identity and aware of my environment, I understood that, although my parents' work lay in Poplar, we were at the same time 'different' from the people amongst whom we lived. *They* were poor, and we had money—not a great deal, but enough; *we* had not to worry about being out of work, or paying the rent, or whether there would be any wages coming in next week. *They* were often hungry, and mostly ill-fed; we were always certain where the next meal was to come from. *They* experienced terrible reversals of fortune: illness, the death of the breadwinner, prolonged unemployment, when everything they possessed was sucked relentlessly into the voracious maw of the pawn-shop, and the inexorable portals of the workhouse gaped for them at the end of the road. We, it seemed, were in comparative control of our own destinies and far less likely to become the helpless playthings of an unmerciful fate; for comfortingly in the background loomed the benevolence and the moderate fortune of my grandparents, sufficient bulwark between ourselves and the shafts of misadventure, against which, I gathered, the poor had few protectors.

In fact, I learned with my alphabet the importance of security; and one of the strongest of my early emotions—apart from family affection—was of gratitude to the Almighty for placing me, by what appeared to be a fortuitous stroke of luck or providence, in such comfortable circumstances. I might have had for parents the roughest of the working-men and the blowsiest of the slatterns whom I saw daily in the streets; for a home, one of the noisome houses into which I would peer fearfully as my pram rolled past the dark recess of an open door. There were even occasional nightmares when I dreamed that I lived in such conditions with such a family, and had lost for ever my own home and people. . . . To wake from these was to know a frightening sense of relief, of escape from evil, and thankfulness to a Deity as yet amorphous.

Children are born snobs. It is only natural to admire the rich, the healthy, the strong and the clever, to despise and reject the poor, the sickly, the struggling and unsuccessful. And yet I must say, in honesty to myself, that I had no feeling of contempt for the unfortunates of Poplar, nor of any conscious superiority, such as would have been only too well in step with the sentiment of the period. I was truly sorry for them. I wished that the children could have good, warm clothing, as I had, and better toys, and something nicer to eat than 'doorsteps'—thick slices of bread smeared with 'marge' or questionable jam; above all, that they need not be beaten, cuffed, and sworn at in the street. I lived, of course, in an atmosphere of continual compassion, hearing my parents talk daily of suffering and the means whereby they might alleviate it. Nevertheless, I was secretly glad not to be as *they* were—not in any pharisaical spirit, but in the sense that from a warm, comfortable room you look out at people driven before the sleet and rain, and are glad to be indoors.

In spite of this natural snobbishness, children do not necessarily appreciate what one must define for lack of a

18

better term as 'class'. This has to be cultivated later, along with a proper social sense and such artificial restraints as disguising your real feelings if they are liable to hurt other people. This is probably why children like to be with gardeners, stablemen, yacht-hands and house-servants, in whose company they feel comfortably free. I was a lonely child, for my sister went away to boarding-school when she was barely eleven, and my parents were naturally much occupied with the work of their enormous parish—in which, for example, the Sunday school alone numbered a thousand children. I was painfully short of playfellows, and I could not for the life of me be made to understand why I must not play with the children in the streets. I could see for myself that they were dirty, their clothes ragged, their hair matted, and their noses constantly running. But some of them were cleaner and better-dressed than others; best of all, they were cheerful, often high-spirited; they screamed with laughter and their pale Cockney cheeks were whipped to redness as they raced along bowling their iron hoops in the sharp wintry air.

Left to play by myself in the Vicarage garden, I would press myself against the railings and stretch my hands between the bars, calling to the children who played outside in what doubtless seemed to me an exhilarating world of freedom and companionship. This democratic behaviour scandalised our servants and was strongly discouraged by Nanny. Eventually a high fence of dark green boards was put up outside the railings, ensuring us a certain amount of privacy and providing the children of the immediate neighbourhood with a ready-made blackboard upon which to scribble untiringly in chalk when they were not engaged in trying to kick it to pieces with their metal-tipped boot-heels.

Although our Vicarage was dull and even ugly, my mother, a passionate and knowledgeable collector of the antique and the lovely, had filled her rooms with some fine pieces of old

19

furniture, which must have looked incongruous, to say the least of it, in their Poplar setting. It was an unrewarding place in which to keep house, for a perpetual and stern campaign had to be carried on against dirt, the chronic dirt of an overcrowded neighbourhood and an industrial city, where the soot from a thousand domestic chimneys combined with the chemical emanations of a score of factories. Curtains and blinds, no less than clothing, had constantly to be washed or cleaned, while acids in the atmosphere destroyed paintwork and undermined bricks and mortar.

Naturally, I saw nothing unusual, or poor, or shabby, about the house. It was my home and therefore familiar, and therefore loved, as any child will love the home where it receives shelter and affection. Indeed, I could find my way about it now, from the moment you get inside the front-door and stand in the narrow hall. Facing you are the stairs, beyond them a door leading to the back regions and ultimately, by a covered passage, to the vestries of the Church. Immediately to the left was my father's study; on the right, at the foot of the stairs, a door opening into a large room which could be divided into two by sliding panels. The rear portion of this room contained a grand piano; but at some time or another it must have been the dining-room, for I remember a dresser lined with china plates, a large table, and, clearest of all, a vision of Elizabeth, the house-parlourmaid, carrying trays of dishes in and out, seen from between the banisters above when I should have been in bed.

The front half of this sensible arrangement could not possibly elude me. It was my mother's drawing-room, filled with fascinating objects against a background of polished walnut and tulip-wood bureaux, of flowery wallpaper, stiff brocaded curtains hung over Nottingham lace, and gilt-framed watercolours, mostly of Italian scenes with cerulean skies or flaming sunsets. There was a carved wooden harem screen, in which the tiny, hinged windows intrigued me enormously; a glass-fronted corner cupboard, picked up for a few pounds in a Welsh village, in which were kept an inexhaustible supply of treasures; an ornamental Venetian boat-hook of sorts, purchased from a gondolier; a wonderful beaten copper fire-screen formed by the outspread tail of a peacock; and a knobkerri, made of wood hard as iron, said to be capable of cracking your skull like an eggshell, and surreptitiously examined by me with ghoulish interest for traces of blood and hair.

This room, in which I repeated the Catechism to my mother on Sunday afternoons, or conversed, stiffly shy, for half an hour or so after tea with visiting 'aunties and uncles', was invested for me with a slight aura of sanctity. Not only had a bishop or two been entertained in there, but a Royal Princess had actually sat in one of the pink and green brocade armchairs and consumed bread and butter and tea within its walls! This august visitor was H.R.H. Princess Christian, who came to open our new Parish Hall in Ullin Street, the building of which was one of the many projects undertaken and achieved by my father with his usual energy, but at no little cost to his health.

It was a red-letter day for everyone connected with the Church—with the possible exception of myself—for visits of Royalty to the East End were not then so frequent as they have since become. So far as I was concerned, it was a day of frustration. I was considered much too young to take any part in the proceedings, but my sister was to be presented to Her Royal Highness. Dressed in her best party-frock, two white satin bows quivering in her long brown hair—for she was trembling with excitement—she was actually summoned to the royal tea-party in the drawing-room while I was obliged to remain, ignored and sulky, in the nursery upstairs. On her return from this moment of triumph, my sister showed me exactly how she had made her curtsey. Although sickened with jealousy, I watched the demonstration fascinated; and for some days afterwards I regarded her right hand with considerable curiosity to discover whether, having been shaken by a hand of the Blood Royal, it had undergone any transformation in its appearance.

Far more familiar than the drawing-room was my father's study, for the highlight of any ordinary week-day was the hour before bedtime that I spent there with him. (On Sundays, the busiest day of the parson's week, we knew that he would be preoccupied and that we could not count on seeing him.) The study always smelt very strongly of tobacco smoke from his pipe, in which he smoked Smith's Glasgow Mixture out of a round wooden jar shaped like a barrel. The smell of this tobacco-jar, rich, aromatic and pungent, was glorious. Time and time again have I savoured it, while my fat fingers, sticky with excitement, delved into its shreddy contents for the promised penny that was so often hidden there.

Perhaps this pipe-smoking was not only a private indulgence but a wise precaution, for the members of my father's flock who called to put up their banns or offer a candidate for confirmation or, far more frequently, to ask his help in some disaster, were not always very well washed. Small wonder, when not 10 per cent of the families in the parish —and 5 per cent is probably nearer the mark—knew the luxury of a bathroom. The East End builder of those days had not progressed very far beyond the mentality of Octavia Hill who, when reporting on flats in the eighteen-sixties, said: 'If you have water on every floor, that is quite sufficient for working people.'

The tobacco smoke thickened into a fog on Monday mornings, when my father held his Chapter, attended by his four curates to discuss every aspect of parochial business. The curates must have been pipe-smokers too, for when they had gone, the smoke lay in heavy blue swathes about the room. My sister and I were not supposed to go near the study on these Monday mornings, but in any case I should have kept

away. Although I was quite accustomed to the fact that
my father, unlike most other people's fathers, often wore
'skirts', I was secretly a little frightened of the curates
in their long, severe black cassocks, their little capes or
voluminous Cowley cloaks, and their birettas: a fear entirely
groundless, for they were the kindest and the most gentle
of men.

The study was a room of enormous fascination to a child.
There were so many things in it that you felt you could
never be done with looking at them all. Its walls were papered
a cosy red; there was a red Turkey carpet, and a great deal
of curiously assorted furniture, which included a whole section
of a racing eight, sliding-seat, stretchers and all, a cottage
piano and a cumbersome musical instrument (now extinct, I
fancy) called a pianola, with which I was to become exceedingly intimate in later years. The top half of the walls was
very nearly covered with reproductions of famous sacred
pictures, such as Mantegna's St George and the beautiful
Madonna of the Sistine Chapel, interspersed with under-
graduate groups bearing the arms of Merton College, Oxford.
Round the bottom half ran rows of shelves containing hundreds
of books, amongst which, as soon as I could read, I would
meditate and browse for hours at a time. They were about
equally divided between my father's major interests: theology
and the sea. On the top of the bookcase and over the mantelpiece stood glass-fronted cases filled with silver cups, vases,
medals and rose-bowls won by my father for rowing and
sailing, and of which I was more inordinately proud than ever
he could have been of winning them.

Above the glass-case on the mantelpiece, high up, far
higher than a small girl could hope to reach, was the most
fascinating object in the room: a fox's mask. It was no chance
acquisition; my father still rode to hounds with the Old
Surrey and Burstow from my grandfather's house in Kent,
being a firm believer in the desirability of taking an occa-

sional day off in the open air from the exactions of such a
parish as St Michael's.

Firm on its wooden shield against the crimson wall the
mask grinned fixedly and perpetually at this alien London
world. It was a fine mask, of a splendid reddish colour—a
dog-fox killed in his prime. Its tawny glass eyes glittered
menacingly, its whiskers, which were liable to become swathed
in cobwebs, stood out stiff and symmetrical on each side of
the snout; sometimes by a shift of the firelight they appeared
to be twitching, especially when the room was in darkness
and my father was telling bedtime stories on winter evenings
by the glow of the flames. The fox's jaws were slightly open,
his black nose was wrinkled to show his bared white teeth
and red, pointed tongue; and—this was the most entrancing
thing of all—tucked in behind the teeth was a halfpenny.
This small copper coin assumed a fantastic importance in my
daily life, for my father would say, mock-serious:

'So long as that ha'penny stays in the fox's mouth, we shall
have money in the bank!'

Very subversive conduct, of course, on the part of a clergyman to foster such idle superstitions in the mind of a child!
I would ask my mother anxiously if it were true, just to hear
her reassuring: 'No, certainly not! It's only your Daddy
joking!'

Nevertheless, I believed him implicitly; a faint, uneasy fear
of penury hovered in the background; the first tiny crack
had appeared in the smooth, strong wall of security which
circumstance had erected between me and the crawling poverty
outside. Automatically, as I marched into the study in agreeable anticipation of an hour's play-time, would I glance up
at the fox's mouth to assure myself that the magic halfpenny
was still there.

And how my father could make my blood run cold, on those
winter evenings after tea, by turning out the study lights and
reciting in fearful tones:

'Hark, hark! The dogs do bark!
The beggars are coming to town!
Some in rags and some in tags,
And some in velvet gown!'

I believe the jingle has either a political or historical
significance which I have forgotten. But I cannot forget to
this day its strange power to make the hair rise on my scalp
and the cold shivers chase themselves down my spine. I could
hear those dogs, far off at first, then coming nearer and nearer
until they were almost in Teviot Street! *Something* had set
them off barking—might it not as well be that evil crew? I
imagined the beggars, like strikers on the march, ragged,
unkempt, some wooden-legged—like Long John Silver—or
one-armed—like Captain Hook—or blind, like Old Pew, tap-
ping and groping their way into town, indescribably sinister,
along the streets from Hackney and Plaistow through Bow
to Poplar. For some reason which, for all I know, may have
been an atavistic one, I always felt that they were approaching
from the north and east; and most dangerous of them all,
because the most mysterious, were the ones 'in velvet gown'!
I could picture their filthy finery, too, greasy and rubbed, like
the pathetic, jet-trimmed capes and jackets that I saw hanging
in the pawnbrokers' windows.

The gas-lamps of Ullin Street threw a sickly greenish light
on the ground-glass panes of a door leading from the study
into the garden. A sudden breeze cast the shadow of a moving
bough upon this pane, thrusting across it like a ragged arm.
. . . I shrieked, and buried my face in my father's waistcoat.
When at last I had been persuaded to unstop my ears and
uncover my eyes, I found him getting a good scolding from
my mother, who had come in from the drawing-room to see
what the screams were about.

'Just before going to bed, too! The child will have
nightmares!'

But I doubt whether I did have nightmares. Upstairs there was always Nanny's reassuring presence, ready with my supper bowl of sugared bread-and-milk, and outside the street-lamps burning brightly, the shops and public-houses lit up as usual, the traffic rumbling by, the children yodelling piercingly to each other from one street-corner to the next—lucky children who never seemed to have to go to bed. And over all, the benign clock-face of St Michael's tower shining warmly through the night.

The day-nursery was easily the best room in the house. Square and bright, it had two large windows facing west towards the railway-line, and two more looking due south, straight down St Leonard's Road. The value of this room as a vantage-point was immense. For one thing, there was an open space in front of the Vicarage, the confluence of streets from all directions. It is occupied now by a Memorial to the men of this parish who gave their lives in the 1914–18 War, but then it provided a focal point for the neighbourhood, a favoured site for open-air meetings, and a gathering-place on high-days and holidays for the admiring crowds that collected to watch the brides and bridegrooms going into church and the newly-wedded couples coming out. Funeral cortèges would drive completely round it in a grand sweep before drawing up at the church door. This was regarded as an essential part of the undertaker's service; without it, the mourning family would feel deprived of their full money's worth. But the principal feature of the place was the pre-dominance of public-houses: there were three within easy hailing distance of each other—and the Vicarage—on the street-corners, and two more in close support further down St Leonard's Road.

Lonely I may have been, but never dull for long, with such an outlook. It was only necessary to kneel up on a chair at one or other of the four nursery windows, and there, for all my waking-hours, was my theatre, puppet-show, and pantomime in one. From breakfast-time until winter-dusk when the curtains were drawn, or the reluctant bedtime of the long, light summer evenings, there was always something to be watched, even if it were only the common currency of street-scenes in the shape of two ragged lads cuffing each other in the gutter, or a runaway milk chariot, the horse's hooves clattering on the road and in its wake a thin blue trail streaming from the milk-churn at the back.

Deplorably but inevitably, the pubs were my main centres of interest. On the pavements outside their ever-open doors could be observed an endless succession of petty dramas, comedies and farces, so many varied aspects of human folly, weakness and forbearance. I do not remember if there were such things as licensing hours. The pubs were certainly functioning well before eight o'clock in the morning, which was roughly when my day began, until long after my bed-time at six or seven o'clock, and I fancy that midnight was their closing hour. On rare occasions, probably Bank Holidays, I would be woken up after many hours of sleep, in what seemed to me the very dead of night, by a fearful commotion in the street outside of shouting, raucous laughter and the tramping of feet. But the calm voice of Nanny would command me to lie down and go to sleep again: it was nothing but the people being turned out of the pubs.

It is scarcely surprising that such places were always well-patronised. Compared to many of the drab little houses, stifling in summer and cheerless in winter, they were at least bright and prosperous-looking, the largest and most substantial buildings in the street. At night their exteriors, often illuminated by the glare of gas-globes, threw broad shafts of light across the dark pavements, for in our part of London, at any rate, the side-streets were poorly lit. Within, the flaring gas-jets shone with the obvious promise of warmth and company on the polished beer-handles, the rows of glasses, and innumerable mirrors.

27

The great London breweries always kept their houses, like their great horse-drawn drays, in very good order, and they were lavishly decorated, receiving a fresh coat of paint once a year, in early summer. The name of the brewery was usually picked out in magnificently ornate lettering with plenty of gold leaf; and my earliest reading-exercises would consist quite often of spelling out such familiar words as 'Charrington's Ales' or 'Mann, Crossman and Paulin'. Some part of the outside was always done in 'graining', and one of the more popular of my free entertainments was to watch the painter wielding a strip of batten to which were fastened three or four brushes, after the manner of an 'impot' writer's multiple-nibbed pen. Dipping each of these in a different-coloured paint, he would delineate with an expert flourish various wavy, irregular markings purporting to represent the grain of marble—such marble as has never been quarried from this earth—upon the good, reliable brown or stone-colour of the pub's doorway.

Round these splendidly sordid portals, at almost any hour of the day but more especially on warm summer afternoons, could be seen a collection of shabby prams and 'go-carts', in which the peaky-faced babies, blue shadows of malnutrition round their closed eyes, the ubiquitous 'dummy' in their mouths, slept uneasily on soiled pillows. If they cried, a sip of stout or the dummy dipped in gin quietened them. The men inside, and the landlord in particular, disliked to hear a pack of squalling brats outside the door; it might remind the customer too forcefully of his domestic responsibilities.

The older children, 'waiting for mother', played listlessly in the gutter, or in wintry weather huddled for warmth round the doorway, peering wistfully now and then into the forbidden place that had such overpowering attractions for their elders. They would be obliged to wait forlornly and with an infinite patience far beyond their years, for hours at a stretch.

I suppose it is an odd admission that I should be ashamed

of making, as well as a reflection on the tendencies of the age, but I would feel distinctly disappointed if during the day I did not see one single drunken person, male or female. Needless to say, this did not often happen!

Directly anyone became too quarrelsome, or so plainly tipsy as to endanger the publican's licence if he should continue to serve them, they were turned out into the street. If enough good sense still prevailed inside their fuddled heads, their mates or wives could manage to get them home without mishap. But only too often the liquor bedevilled them into arguments, and the arguments stung them into fighting. How ridiculous they looked, I would think, as they stood about in the road regardless of the traffic, swaying on their feet, getting as red in the face as turkey-cocks, mouthing at each other with glares of silly fury! They would tap each other on the chest to mark their words; the tap would become a push that made the other stagger; he would retaliate with a wild swing, and the fight was on, until someone with a cooler head contrived to separate them, or make them understand that a policeman was in sight. The 'coppers' on those beats must have been highly experienced, for they were capable of judging to a nicety when to walk past with an averted eye and when it was necessary to interfere.

After a time I, too, developed a kind of instinct, an embryo ability to tell when a fight was going to peter out or flare up into a scrap worth watching: a curious accomplishment for the daughter of a parson. When real trouble was brewing a crowd always collected, springing up apparently from beneath the paving-stones. With the Cockney's natural sense of fairness and a deep-rooted feeling that it was 'better to let them fight it out', a ring would be formed, and rigorously kept, in that convenient open space before the Vicarage gates.

These sort of fights invariably ended in the intervention of a police-constable, for when matters had gone to the length of squaring up to each other in the ring, the contestants were far gone in drink and meant business. But, like most East Enders, they were practised in the rudiments of pugilism, and so long as they could keep on their feet, they would make a fair show of 'covering up' and taking passably scientific hooks and swings at each other.

The crowd always goaded them on with encouraging cries, and if any women were among the onlookers, their shrill yells would rise clearly to my nursery window, which would probably be wide open by this time, for Nanny herself was not above taking a shocked peep at the disgraceful business. Blood would be drawn, and tempers start to rise, although I doubt if the damage ever amounted to much more than cut lips, black eyes and bleeding noses. Then, like magic, the outer fringes of the crowd would melt away; a 'copper' could be seen shouldering his way without haste but with determination through the circle, and the average person in our neighbourhood considered it plain common sense not to let the police remember your existence, or at least your presence at that particular spot on that particular day. Within a minute or so the open space would be clear, and nothing remain of the incident but the solid blue back of the constable disappearing down the street accompanied by both the crestfallen brawlers on their way to be charged at the station in the East India Dock Road.

Fortunately it was rare, though not unknown, to see two women fighting, for when they did it was a vile spectacle. The degradation of women seemed correspondingly lower than the degradation of men. Even I, a child, was made aware of it, as much from my own sensations of disgust as from the brutish, half-ashamed expressions on the faces of the spectators.

The women fought most often on Bank Holidays when, I suppose, they had celebrated their temporary freedom from household drudgery by getting very drunk. Unluckily, they would then be wearing their best clothes, which were even more unsuitable for violent action than their everyday uniform of rusty black skirt dragging on the ground behind, dirty apron, leg-of-mutton-sleeved jacket or ancient cape, and masculine cloth cap anchored to the bun of hair by hat-pins; and inevitably it would be an affair of something more than fisticuffs. Down in the dust would go the huge, be-feathered cartwheel hats of ceremony, handfuls of hair would be torn out, a bedraggled feather boa wrenched in half, flounces ripped from the trailing Edwardian skirts which they lifted knee-high in the attempt to get an unhampered kick at an opponent, especially if she, poor wretch, had tripped over a torn hem and fallen. They fought savagely and unfairly, slapping, scratching, and biting; and their wild shrieks of rage and pain sounded as though the very last shreds of self-control had left them. There was always the danger then that they would use their long hat-pins on each other's eyes. The police hated handling these furies, and never seemed to be on the spot when needed; often a man would be driven to step out of the crowd and put an end to the sickening performance by clamping the woman's elbows together behind her back. But that did not necessarily dam the flow of her screaming vituperation.

Occasionally a husband and wife would choose to wash their domestic dirty linen in public, but such quarrels seldom developed beyond the stage of violent altercations. If they came to blows, it was not invariably the man who got the best of it. A little game-chicken of a woman who kept dancing in to hit her big husband when and where she could impressed herself indelibly on my infant memory. She was in her working clothes and had sufficient freedom of action to keep out of his grasp. He was tipsy enough to be staggering, and at first he did not know how to deal with her. Eventually, exasperated, he took off his heavy leather belt and began to beat her unmercifully with the buckle end—the normal East End instrument of chastisement. Her howls rang out until a policeman appeared. The husband, now thoroughly aroused, resisted the constable in the execution of his duty, and the 'copper' was obliged to put a half-nelson on him. Instantly the woman stopped nursing her sore ribs, and tugging at the hat-pin with which her cloth cap was skewered to her hair, sprang forward like a tigress. But it was the policeman at whom she stabbed, and she aimed at his eyes. The shrill blast of a police-whistle—common sound on our streets—rose in the air, and the wounded constable was led away bleeding by a colleague. Somewhat shaken by this sudden drama, I watched them hustling the woman away as well; she looked small and singularly defenceless in the massive clutch of the law, her torn apron blowing out with a last frivolously defiant flutter.

The affair was debated with some spirit by Nanny, Mrs Owers, the nursery char, and myself. We felt that she had been more sinned against than sinning, though of course it was very wrong to stab a policeman with your hat-pin. Whether she was one of my father's parishioners whom he would have visited in prison—for she, at any rate, must have 'gone to college' for a while—or whether Mrs Owers had picked up a piece of gossip, I do not remember; but by some means we heard that, when charged, the woman had said in her own defence that 'she couldn't abear to see the copper knockin' 'er old man abaht'. She had only been trying to get him out of the pub before he spent all the week's wages: a purely domestic affair in which the police had no right to interfere.

Thus I learned at an early age the useful truth that drink, like fire, is a good servant but a bad master, although its attraction remained as incomprehensible to me as to any of the unfortunate children cooling their heels outside the 'boozer'. To drink for the sake of drinking until you had to come outside and be sick in the gutter struck me as an over-rated pastime. As if that was not enough to put you off the stuff for the time being, you went back into the pub for more.

True, such behaviour mostly occurred on Bank Holidays, when the people crowded into the pubs the whole day long, and I enjoyed what would be called in the jargon of today my peak-periods of pub-watching. We children were not allowed out on these occasions, for the streets were considered to be too rowdy. We were marooned in the Vicarage as on an island, while the tides of East End life, rough and noisy, washed round the blackened brick walls of our shabby abode and the sooty little garden.

Enthralling though the puppet-show might be, I was always glad when the holiday was over, and we could sally forth once more into the adventurous world beyond the Vicarage gates.

2. East of Aldgate Pump

'GOING to college' was a euphemism taken quite literally
to begin with by my mother, who felt gratified that a proportion, however small, of the parishioners had such studious
inclinations.

How many of them were habitual or casual criminals I
have no idea. Certainly the parish contained 'bad' streets, the
black spots of the district, into which the police were said
never to penetrate at night and always in pairs by day. My
father visited in them, naturally; and Nanny, who was an
indefatigable walker, pushing me in my pram and later hauling me on my short, fat legs up and down the length and
breadth of the parish and beyond, was quite fearless into the
bargain, and went down any street she had a mind to. But
the parson's kid and her nurse, like the parson himself, were
known to everyone and possessed the best safe-conduct in the
whole of London: they were above suspicion as 'copper's
narks'.

Many of these back-streets, however, were highly respectable, and considering the district, comparatively pleasant,

save for the monotony of the endless repetitive bay-windows, each tightly closed summer and winter alike, heavily draped in bobble-fringed plush and the inevitable Nottingham lace, parted just sufficiently to show the best ornamental vase or china figure displayed on a small table covered with a bright sateen cloth. Sometimes the space between the curtains would be occupied almost entirely by a fern, aspidistra or climbing-plant in a large bowl: a ruse employed, according to the nasty-minded, to hide the fact that there was little furniture left in the room behind!

The house-fronts, which boasted some attempt at decoration in the shape of a little fancy brickwork or plaster acanthus leaves over the lintels, were separated from the pavements by iron railings enclosing the area-steps, for most of these 'superior' terraces had basements. In summer there would be a fine display of window-boxes, for the East Ender of those days rated horticulture as a pastime on only a slightly lower level than that of keeping pets. Being as yet denied the benefits of football-pools, the cinema—although there was a smelly 'Picturedrome' in the East India Dock Road—wireless and television, he was a great 'fancier', and employed his leisure a great deal more productively with his whippets, rabbits and pigeons, as though the last vestiges of his country inheritance still struggled for expression.

Their back-gardens were a wonderful example of concentrated cultivation in the face of difficulties; the little patch of stale town earth would be induced to grow not only flowers, but a row or two of runner beans and radishes, a tiny square of sooty grass, and perhaps an 'arbour', formed by training Virginia creeper with painstaking care across one corner of the garden, where one or two chairs could be placed on hot summer evenings to produce an illusion of privacy and shade. Along the house-wall would be ranged the rabbit-hutches, the cramped cages where a thrush or linnet could barely stretch its wings, and the universal long tin tub in which the family

took their baths. Life in such a street was not too difficult;
here the bugbear of want was at least kept at arm's length by
its inhabitants, who would include those aristocrats of the
district, the railwaymen. It was easy to understand that they
preferred such homes to the great new blocks of council flats
then beginning to rise as the first-fruits of slum clearance
schemes, in which, the people bitterly complained, they could
not keep their pets nor dig their bits of gardens.

But there were bleak courts of stark poverty and hopeless
outlook, the houses dwarfed and vision blocked by the high
brick wall of a factory or the arch of a railway viaduct, lit at
night by a single lamp-post set in the broken pavement
around which the children swung perpetually on frayed ends
of rope.

There were long, straight avenues of the cheapest kind of
hovel in which men could be induced to live, run up by
speculative builders at the worst period of the industrial expan-
sion to house the lowest-paid workers, where the terrible
sameness was intensified by the absence of any relief in the
featureless vista of frontages. The dreary stretches of brick,
pierced by the necessary apertures for doors and windows,
rose direct from the pavements to the low parapet which con-
cealed the mean roof, consisting of a single gable, provided
for each dwelling. The parallel lines of kerbstone, house-front
and parapet running along together and converging in the
middle distance, conveyed an effect of deadening and dreadful
inescapability, as powerful in the sullen, veiled sunshine of an
airless summer's day as in the cold saffron murk of a November
twilight.

The front-doors opened over a level threshold immediately
upon a living-room, which only too often revealed the boards
of a floor without covering, walls bare save for discoloured
patches of greasy dirt or damp, furniture consisting of little
save packing-cases and a heap of indescribable cloths in one
corner. If there were small children in the house, a rough

wooden partition thrust into the bottom of the doorway kept them from toddling out into the street. Pinned into faded rags, their hair matted, their noses running, these poor babies peered indifferently over the planks that barricaded them into their noisome homes. It was to visit houses such as these that my father would change into a special suit that was never even brought into our part of the Vicarage; in such a house that my mother once watched the walls glistening and shimmering, mistaking the effect for an odd sort of iridescent wallpaper until she realised with a shock that it was *alive* and crawling with vermin.

Here lay the very heart of the parochial problem. How was it possible for these people to retain their self-respect or respond with any fervour to the exhortations of their parish priest when some iron law of circumstance had depressed them to such a way of living? At the beginning of the twentieth century we were but fifty years removed from Mayhew and his times; my father's parishioners were but the children and grandchildren of the people he described: the mudlarks, the dust-pickers, the crossing-sweepers and the pure-finders. Many of them scarcely knew of a better standard of life even if it had been possible to attain it; they were barely aware of the steady flood-tide of improvement in their condition which had already begun to seep into every nook and cranny of the social structure, even if they had heard the names of Will Crooks and George Lansbury.

They still lived terrifyingly close to the edge of destitution. They had no china ornaments to display in their front-windows; the windows themselves were seldom whole, the broken panes stuffed with rags or newspapers, and almost everything portable in the home paid periodic visits to the pawnbroker's. It was said that you could judge exactly how close to poverty a family had come by what they hung out on the line each washing-day. The better-off would still have bed-linen—one of the first things to find its way to 'uncle's';

the poorest had but a few rags of clothing, not easily identi-
fiable. Their children went barefoot in the mud and slush of
winter as well as in the dust of summer. They had little or
no underclothing; through the tears in their jackets or dresses
you usually saw flesh. Most horrifying of all, from November
to March they were sewn securely into layers of brown paper
in lieu of winter woollens, rather as a peasant-child was once
coated in goose-fat.

In these streets it was no uncommon thing to come upon
the scene of final degradation—the bailiff's men piling on a
single cart the few shillings' worth of sticks and crocks which
represented the sum total of these people's worldly goods,
while the man and woman thus dispossessed stood by to
watch them go with no other show of emotion beyond a
sullen indifference or at most a futile defiance. Nor could I
ever grow sufficiently hardened to pass unmoved the melancholy spectacle of an elderly couple standing dejectedly outside
the pawn-shop, staring with reddened eyes at some precious
article inside.

'When they're old like that,' it was explained to me, 'and
their home's gone, they haven't much hope of redeeming the
things again.'

No one could ever have claimed that our Poplar streets
were dull. Mean, shabby, dreary they may have been, but
never uneventful. Some large houses still stood towards the
western end of the East India Dock Road that must have
looked handsome enough in their heyday, when they had
sheltered substantial, even prosperous, middle-class families
connected with the Indies trade; but it was the inhabitants
of the district, rather than the architecture, to whom one
turned for interest. Daily I rubbed shoulders with Negroes,
Lascars, Arabs and Chinese—and was astonished to learn in
later life that the colour of a person's skin was regarded by
some people as ample cause to place him outside the brother-
hood of man. In the main they were seafarers, excepting the

Chinese, who formed a considerable colony of their own mostly concentrated round 'Charlie Brown's Corner' and the West India Dock Road. Their blue-clad figures moving along the crowded pavements, wet or fine, with an unhurried shuffle, looked a good deal more Oriental than do their modern counterparts today even in the setting of a Far Eastern city, for at that time they wore the pigtail almost to a man. Their womenfolk one seldom saw, but there would be plenty of half-caste children playing in the gutter whose blue eyes stared up at you incongruously out of almond-shaped slits. Chinamen were reputed to make excellent husbands, less addicted to drink and wife-beating than Englishmen!

Some of the huge, flat Chinese faces had a mottled greenish pallor, like unripe gorgonzola cheese, or the full moon seen through a thin fog. Nanny and I firmly believed these unfortunates, who were plainly sick, to be opium-smokers. I have no idea upon what grounds we based this piece of unshakeable dogma, but it was an undisputed fact that there were opium-dens in the turnings off the West India Dock Road. Indeed, my father had actually run to earth an errant member of his flock in one of these unsavoury places, which were as far removed, I imagine, from the glamorous and exotic halls depicted on the West End stage as a common lodging-house from the Ritz Hotel. The story of how my father had found and rescued this straying sheep was one I often clamoured to be told in that pre-bedtime hour in the fire-lit study, however familiar I might have been already with each enthralling detail about grunting Chinamen, insensible forms in tiers of bunks, tiny black balls of opium sizzling away over little lamps, and the somewhat unromantic fact that it had not been very difficult to get the man away.

Twenty years later, exploring the less reputable parts of Calcutta city, I recognised a sickly, sweet-sour aroma as something wonderfully reminiscent of—what? 'Smell the opium?' someone murmured; and instantly I was back in the

West India Dock Road among the cheese-faced Chinamen!

Then there were the drunks, whom we learned not to fear, and never obviously to avoid. People who stopped to stare or drew back ostentatiously with loud expressions of horror or disgust at such behaviour only had themselves to thank if they attracted the unwelcome attentions of the inebriated. So long as you minded your own business and walked past them as unconcernedly as though there were nothing in the least unusual about them, they were harmless enough.

In any case they were unavoidable, for it was quite impossible to leave or enter the Vicarage without passing several pubs. 'How terrible for you,' lamented our friends from the fashionable world, 'to live in this atmosphere of perpetual drunkenness!' I found their sympathy puzzling. I was never reluctant to go past a pub; if anything, I tried to loiter. I rather liked to hear the jolly, boozy singing that issued from these interesting establishments, although when the East Ender was fairly drunk, the singing became more and more lugubrious, the women's strident voices in particular revelling in the long-drawn-out melancholy of those soulful ditties. If the doors were open in warm weather, I liked to catch a glimpse of the interior: the floor, newly sprinkled with bran or sawdust; the tall black glasses of stout topped with rich cream froth, and the mahogany clarity of beer; the astounding array of bottles behind the formidable barmaid, whose crimped and puffed hair stuck full of ornamental combs glittered splendidly as she served the customers, pulling powerfully and swiftly at the rows of pump-handles before her. And outside the pubs stood knots of women, drinking their stout or gin and chatting sociably on the pavement. They had a habit —which I do not mind admitting intrigued me greatly—of relieving nature by the simple process of straddling the gutter while the conversation and the drinking went on uninterrupted. I do not recall that I was ever shocked by this uninhibited conduct. Nanny, of course, would hurry us on, clicking her tongue distractedly; but even she could not manage to divert my attention from the universal and revolting custom of spitting, and of using the pavement in lieu of a pocket-handkerchief.

Whenever I cried in the street or behaved tiresomely, Nanny would employ her usual threat to 'take me to the police station' or, as a last resort, to 'give me to Old Mother Bunch'. Old Mother Bunch was a half-demented, destitute creature, a shapeless bundle of rusty black from the ancient bonnet perched on her scanty hair to the tattered pelisse about her shoulders and the voluminous skirts in which the gaping rents were held together by large safety-pins. She was filthy and stinking, and her poverty-stricken aspect excited morbid curiosity as to how, and where, she managed to exist at all. She trundled aimlessly along the gutters, muttering to herself, her bloodshot eyes darting from side to side, stooping now and then to pick up cigarette-ends, cabbage-stalks and bread-crusts. Sometimes a policeman 'moved her on', and then she stood and screamed incomprehensible abuse at him. I could not bring myself to believe entirely that Nanny would really hand me over into the keeping of this repellent and terrifying hag, and grown-up people, I had discovered, did not always mean exactly what they said; but the dread of this misfortune was quite enough to stop any normal flow of tears.

Since, with inexorable regularity, Nanny and I went for a walk twice every weekday, and nothing save rain, a pea-soup fog, or the incidence of Bank Holidays was allowed to interfere with this programme, we came to know the district intimately. I enjoyed going out for walks as much as any West End child whose feet trod the select pavements of Kensington, whose fresh air was unpolluted by such vulgar stenches as the vile smells given off by factories or the clouds of greasy fumes that belched from the numerous fried fish shops. No gleaming chromium plate or shining white-tiled walls embellished such places then; you preferred not to look too long into the rancid depths of those fœtid, dark interiors. As for the factory stinks, you could tell quite easily from which quarter the wind was blowing merely by sniffing, the cardinal points of the compass identifying themselves faithfully by a particular smell: west, horseflesh (for dog-biscuits); north, sulphur-fumes (for matches); north-east, fish manure; and due east, the pungent stench of a paint-works, with gas thrown in for good measure. A certain bridge over Limehouse Cut, in fact, was known as Stink Bridge; few names were better deserved, and I never heard or knew that it had any other.

To the north of St Michael's a web of uninteresting streets gradually frayed out into a noxious growth of specially malodorous factories which had grown up over what had once been the pretty village of Bow clustering round the spot where Queen Matilda first spanned the River Lea with her famous bridge. Industrialism had blighted utterly this triangle formed by the junction of the Limehouse Cut and Bow Creek, as the reaches of the Lea below Old Ford were known. So far as I can remember, the only reason we had for traversing this dismal region was an invitation to have tea with the Matron of Bromley Hospital, who happened to be an extremely devout member of my father's congregation. The experience was a little awe-inspiring. In spite of the excellence of the tea and the gratifyingly grown-up level of the conversation, which usually covered such adult subjects as the quality of the curates' sermons, Lenten penances, Confession, and the iniquities of the Kensitites, I was always relieved to escape from Matron's spotless sitting-room, in which the disquieting hospital smells of ether and disinfectant could still be detected faintly. I was always afraid that, by some odd mischance, I might be detained in one of the huge, bare, shining wards into which we glanced as Matron saw us off the premises.

To the south, down the length of St Leonard's Road, lay the great thoroughfare of the neighbourhood, the East India

Dock Road: the roaring river of trade, traffic and people, the artery along which the life-blood of commerce streamed between the Docks and London itself. Over its granite setts the huge, horse-drawn drays and wagons of London's heaviest transport rumbled and clattered; the tall trams swayed and whined down the centre of its considerable width. Eastward from the triple-arched gateway of the Docks and the incongruous red entrance to the Blackwall Tunnel, past Poplar Hospital, where the patients in their scarlet flannel jackets took the air in fine weather on the balconies, and All Hallows Church, the road ran on towards Canning Town. This we regarded as an uninteresting walk: a terrace of bay-windowed houses on the one hand, on the other the long, black, unbroken wall of the Docks, above which could be seen the topmasts and upper yards of sailing-ships, the smoke of steamers, and crane-jibs moving intelligently to and fro as of their own volition.

But Nanny and I had certain interests in Canning Town. The shops in the High Street were very good, and Nanny actually had a friend who kept a confectioner's just beyond the station, opposite to what is now the junction with Silvertown Way. Here I was in the habit of buying Everton Toffees, which I liked best, and Hundreds-of-Thousands, which I considered a good return for my money although I did not much care for their insipid flavour. And it was here, in Canning Town—a name for ever linked in my mind with social discomfiture—that I suffered the humiliation of falling through the bottom of my pram; for, of course, to begin with my walks were in reality pram-rides.

Of all places, it happened on the very crown of the old Iron Bridge; Fate could hardly have picked a more conspicuous spot on which to stage such a disaster. Doubtless I had been bouncing up and down, plaguing Nanny to let me get out, for the sight of the paving-stones rolling smoothly by beneath my wheels would excite in me an urgent desire to walk on them; and the old pram, which my sister had used before me, could not stand up to this treatment for ever, especially as I grew larger and heavier. Nanny had just pushed me up the incline of the bridge when there was an ominous rending sound and the bottom of the pram fell out. Not only was it painful, it was alarming; besides, I felt deeply humiliated, and began to cry with the full force of a pair of lungs that had never been feeble. Everybody, I imagined, in Poplar, Bromley and Bow, not to mention Canning Town, would point me out in future as the little girl who fell through the bottom of her pram going over the Iron Bridge. To make matters worse, I was obliged to trudge home beside the disreputable, discredited object which was being pushed crossly along by Nanny, its splintered floor hanging down so that everyone could see what had happened.

The old Iron Bridge has been replaced by a wide, impersonal, modern structure of reinforced concrete, and its approaches have been altered out of all recognition by the bombs of the Luftwaffe; nevertheless to this day I undergo a slight depression of the spirit whenever I drive across it—as in later years I have had regular occasion to do on my way to and from the Docks—as though that disastrous afternoon had left a permanent imprint upon my inner consciousness.

This association of ideas is both strong and abiding. I still imagine, in spite of up-to-date evidence to the contrary, that Burdett Road is highly sinister because it used to contain a shop with the word 'Apothecary' above a secretive and dirty window filled with wire screening that prevented one from looking in. The most odious stench pervaded the place, and nothing would convince me that they were not concocting horrible medicines inside, of which the principal ingredients were extracted from dead bodies. A street to be avoided! So, too, was Brunswick Road where, as I walked unsuspectingly beneath a block of flats, an iron-spiked top thrown or spun accidentally from a balcony struck me on the fleshy part of the eye, provoking cries of pain, anger and outrage even more piercing than on the distressing occasion of the Canning Town catastrophe.

Abbott Road, on the other hand, although long and monotonous, was a much more favoured thoroughfare along which Nanny and I passed regularly to call at Christie's Electric Printing Works. Here the Parish Magazine was printed, and month by month we would deliver into Mr Christie's ink-stained hands the fresh material or the corrected proofs. Small wonder that I liked to visit Abbott Road! It was Mr Christie himself who, in the year 1910, produced with the utmost care a novel written by myself: a full-blooded romance entitled *Hazel Care* after its heroine, a high-minded if adventurous girl who, having survived a series of mishaps calculated to daunt a Dick Barton, finally marries a nauseatingly smug hero called Rupert Somerville, despite the machinations of one Martin Judkins, the villainous son of a farmer—conclusive evidence there, I fancy, of the deep-rooted suspicion nourished in the bosoms of the city-bred towards all countrymen.

Gravely we consulted over the format of *Hazel Care*, in a strong atmosphere of printers' ink with the presses of the Electric Printing Works rumbling away threateningly in the background. Mr Christie, a tired-looking man with iron-grey moustaches, a kindly smile, and his cloth cap pushed to the back of his head, took immense pains to find appropriate illustrations. There is a frontispiece of Hazel herself (with a distinctly Victorian hair-do); Rupert is represented (rather to my annoyance) as a plump schoolboy in knickerbockers and an Eton collar; while on the last page, suitably enough, there is a drawing of a splendid wedding-cake. The whole is bound in red paper, lettered in gilt and tied with yellow cord; at sixpence it sold like hot cakes in aid of parish funds at the annual Church Bazaar that year.

The East India Dock Road, followed westwards, was a

more varied and profitable proposition than that portion of it leading east to Canning Town. To go along it as far as Charlie Brown's corner, and home by the West India Dock Road and Poplar High Street was a very favourite circular route of ours. Among its attractions I rated the statue of Mr George Green, the celebrated shipbuilder, on his pedestal outside the Poplar Baths. Mr Green did not interest me greatly, but I much admired the very life-like image of a dog at his feet: as true a portrait, I imagine, as that of the man himself.

Then there was St Matthias's Church, original chapel of the Honourable East India Company, in which I took a certain proprietary interest on learning that one of my mother's family had served that august body for many years in India. The church still preserves a curiously rural appearance, its interior made remarkable by the shiny brown pillars that were once the masts of ships. Local legend declared them to have belonged to the defeated Spanish Armada, but in plain truth they were nothing more romantic than the masts of old Indiamen extracted, as a dentist pulls an ancient fang, at the Brunswick Mast House at Blackwall when the ships were broken up.

Nearly opposite St Matthias was another landmark of great importance to myself. This was the famous bookshop of Mr Seager, whose books must have circumnavigated the globe several times over in the cabins and libraries of countless ships. In those days I knew nothing of this; but I must have spent many happy hours in there, choosing drawing-books, writing-paper, crayons and pencils, while often Mr Seager himself, gently smiling and the soul of patience, waited for me to make up my mind.

A little further along on the same side of the East India Dock Road, just beyond the railway line as you came from the eastward, was a magnet of irresistible attraction: the Chrisp Street Market. It is one of the celebrated street-

markets of London, probably only less familiar to the outer
world than Petticoat Lane because it is less easily accessible.
It consisted in our time of nothing more than a double row
of stalls under canvas tilts lining the short, narrow street,
but it held for me a perennial fascination; there were few
prospects that pleased me more than Nanny's announcement
that we were to go shopping in Chrisp Street. Certain things
we bought there regularly, for they were not to be found
anywhere else in the neighbourhood, nor so cheap. In early
summer there would be a serious expedition to buy bedding-
out plants for that important project, my garden; just before
Christmas it was necessary to buy small presents and decorations for the Tree—the kind of thing that today one finds at
Woolworth's.

That was the time to see it in all the height of its glory and
bustle, on an afternoon in late December, when a leaden sky
pressed down low over the chimney-tops and a chill east wind
blew a murky haze up from the River. In the early winter
dusk the naphtha flares had long been lit, their flames blowing
out wildly like fluttering yellow hands and casting a brilliant,
hypnotic glare upon the faces of the crowds gathered round
each stall. In this fierce illumination the wares displayed
looked considerably more inviting than in the cold light of
day. I lingered lovingly before mounds of sickly-coloured
sweets and groves of candy-pink rock, none of which was I
allowed to buy, since Nanny maintained that all cheap confectionery was made with glucose and therefore unwholesome
—an opinion widely held in those days.

There were bales of shoddy materials in the vivid shades
so dear to East End hearts—blue, violet, magenta, carmine;
and gaudy oleographs, both sacred and profane—for a few
pence you could decorate the walls of a small room in the
crudest primary colours and only the poorest homes were
without such pictures.

Over the hardware stalls the brightest lights of all were

reflected on the shining tin pots and pans, the cheap white china, the coloured and gilded vases set out so temptingly to divert a shilling or two from the housewife's purse. Indeed, you could furnish a home in Chrisp Street, for whole suites of rough deal furniture—'thrown together' as Nanny scornfully described it—stood about on the pavement, together with rolls of carpet and shiny, beflowered oilcloth.

But the food-stalls were the principal attraction and drew the densest crowds. The butcher in his blue coat and blue-and-white striped apron stood framed against a background of red-and-white joints, sharpening his long knives and crying the excellence of his meat. He sold all sorts of interesting pieces never served at the nursery table, such as calves' heads, cow's heel, brains, pigs' trotters, faggots, chitterlings, not to mention tripe, liver and lights. Cheapest cuts were two-pence a pound—'trimmings', which my mother bought, often out of her own pocket, to make great cauldrons of meat-stew for the women and children of the parish in times of great hardship and distress caused by a prolonged strike or lock-out.

Still more interesting, if repulsive, were the live eels writhing slowly together on the fishmongers' trays, and their dead jellied counterparts—a prime delicacy—and the piles of shellfish to be eaten on the spot with the help of plenty of vinegar and pepper, and the traditional pin. I longed to taste them. It seemed to me a highly enjoyable experience to stand there in the glare of the sizzling naphtha eating your whelks and chatting to the woman who sold them. But Nanny ordained with unwavering bigotry that such things were 'common', and said that I could buy them if I liked when I was grown-up: a period in time so distant as not to be worth bothering about.

Pyramids of oranges, and russet apples polished to a startling degree—by spitting on them, we always understood —made patches of brilliant, warming colour on the fruit-stalls. You could buy good oranges for a halfpenny each, and some were four a penny—but these might have been bruised or over-ripe. The weather might be bitter, their bare hands and feet purple with cold, nevertheless the children bought oranges eagerly, tearing them apart and eating them with avidity on the spot, down to the last shred of peel, as though the fruit supplied some urgent need in their scanty diet. They even devoured lemons in the same fashion, apparently with enjoyment, although the mere sight screwed one's mouth up uncontrollably. Here again I was hampered by petty decorum, being allowed to eat an orange only at the table, accompanied by a plate and a spoon; admittedly the skin, when I tried it surreptitiously, merely tasted nasty. Roast chestnuts were different, although we preferred to take these home raw and cook them on the bars of the nursery fire. In Chrisp Street the glowing red eye of the chestnut-seller's brazier gleamed fitfully through the shifting figures that pressed round it; for even if you could not afford a pennyworth, you could warm yourself for nothing at the red-hot metal and savour the rich roasting smell before the vendor chased you away to make room for more profitable customers.

The noise was continuous; everyone bawled their wares in raucous yelps or long wailing cries. People thrust their way through the throng in search of a special purchase, or crowded round a cheapjack with a ready tongue and powerful lungs, selling half-crown watches or a bottle of medicine, panacea for every ill, at the price of sixpence. As darkness fell this short avenue of allurement, where every stall formed a kind of smoky, golden Aladdin's cave, became more vociferous and congested. The excitement of the whole place intensified enormously; unfortunately, at the same time, Nanny's thoughts would turn with the certitude of clockwork towards nursery tea, and we would hurry back to the respectable seclusion of the Vicarage via the convenient short-cut of Grundy Street.

The brief length of Chrisp Street is now bare of stalls and

lit on dark, windy winter nights by nothing less prosaic than ordinary street-lamps. The Market itself has been incorporated in the nearby Lansbury Housing Estate on the recommendation of some enthusiastic and ingenious architect. It is all very neat and comfortably under cover and a vast improvement; but in some curious, inexplicable way the planners have defeated their own ends. Years later, driving back from a ship in London Docks, the taxi-driver took me round that way to avoid congestion in the East India Dock Road. He was a Poplar man himself, born and bred in Ida Street; and when I commented on the transformation of the Chrisp Street Market, he complained with unexpected bitterness:

'All the heart seems to have gone out of it! You just walk round and round and there's no fun in it any more.'

That is the very last thing that could have been said of it some fifty years ago; and I could tell that a deep-rooted local patriotism had been affronted, an injury with which I could feel a certain sympathy. At some very early age I began to develop a sentiment of affectionate loyalty, which has never died away entirely, for the familiar surroundings of Poplar. When I was no more than six or maybe seven I was taken to see some relatives of my mother's who lived in one of those majestic, frozen terraces to the north of Oxford Street. I can merely recall that the house had an imposing portico over the front-door and a first-floor drawing-room with immensely tall french windows opening on to a wide road that seemed to me oddly deserted after the swarming pavements of the East End. Someone very slim and elegant with grey hair piled on the top of her head rose to greet us.

'Why, is *this* the slum-child?' she exclaimed, when I was gently pushed forward from the shelter of my mother's skirts. 'But she's got rosy cheeks—*quite* wrong!'

I was enormously offended. Some aspersion had been cast upon Poplar, although in what way I could not have defined.

Some defence, I felt, was needed of the place that I had become accustomed to regard as home; yet I did not know how to make it. After luncheon other children had been invited to come and play with me—children from 'up-West', as we said in our part of the world, which by a natural inversion implied that we lived 'down-East', although I never heard it described as such. I behaved badly the whole afternoon, became rough and rude, told lies, boasted and bragged in a way that the other children clearly, but politely, found distasteful. They beat me at games—I explained, as off-hand as possible, that I simply was not trying. Two of them performed some successful conjuring tricks—elementary enough, I daresay, yet I could not see how they were done. Not to be outshone, I asserted doggedly that I had supernatural powers and could make fairies appear—only I did not choose to exert myself just then. In the train going home, grinding and jolting to a halt at all the grimy, gas-lit stations between Broad Street and South Bromley—Dalston Junction, Homerton, Haggerston, Hackney and Bow—my mother rebuked me for my behaviour; I had made her thoroughly ashamed of me. Normally I should have dissolved into floods of tears at a far more temperate reproof, but for once I was unrepentantly defiant. I had given, I knew, the most deplorable exhibition of bad manners; but at least they would not easily forget the slum-child!

3. The Finest Playground in London

DAMP and foggy from the River, laden with chemical impurities, the East End air did not suit my sister and she was soon translated from the comfortable orbit of our nursery world to the strange and almost grown-up life of boarding school. By contrast, the lack of open spaces, the smoke-filled atmosphere and over-crowded streets seemed positively to agree with me. The elegant lady in West London had been perfectly correct about my rosy cheeks; my appearance failed entirely to conform to the conventional idea of what a child should look like whose growing years had been spent in that region of unimaginable squalor east of Aldgate Pump!

True, I was subject each winter to attacks of bronchitis, in spite of enforced doses of such detested medicines as a glutinous white emulsion, or chemical food and cod liver oil mixed nauseously together in a china spoon; the liberal external application of camphorated oil and the wearing of a curious waistcoat manufactured by Nanny out of rolls of cotton-wool.

One year my winter scourge developed into congestion of the lungs. My chest hurt and I felt languid; but not so languid that I failed to appreciate my elevation to a new importance in the normal household life. My bed was moved into the day-nursery; a strange nurse arrived to look after me whose ministrations I rejected strongly even as a partial substitute for Nanny's. Never for one moment did I feel ill enough to contemplate the possibility of dying, but from time to time I asked the nurse whether straw had been put down in Ullin Street—for I had seen this done outside a house where some-one was lying 'at death's door'—and felt vaguely defrauded when she invariably replied: 'Oh, dear me, no! You're not nearly bad enough for that!' with horrible professional jauntiness.

Of course she was speaking the truth, for my principal memory is not of pain but of exasperation at being unable to see what was going on outside. My sister's visits infuriated me still further. Home for the holidays, perfectly well and free to walk about, she would gaze out of the window— instead of remaining sympathetically at the patient's bedside —and torment me by affecting a lively interest in what was happening in the street. I would implore her to tell me what she saw—drunks?—a fight?—a fallen horse?—an accident? She would answer enigmatically, and saunter out of the room with a maddening smile, as of one who had just witnessed an unusually amusing or exciting spectacle, to return to her superior adolescent occupations downstairs.

Possibly she had only been pretending, for at that time she never tired of teasing me relentlessly. Five years, when one of you is six and the other eleven, is a chasm hard to bridge; our relationship was inevitably one of patronage and supplica-tion, and doubtless my infantile importunings were often tiresome. Not until we were both grown-up did the truth emerge that we were deeply attached to one another—when our age discrepancy had levelled up and there was no longer much concrete virtue in the statement: 'Please remember that I am your *elder* sister!'

The nurse, Nanny, Mrs Owers, the nursery cleaner, all did their utmost to keep me in touch with events by pains-taking descriptions of the scene outside; but I could not visualise such sights vicariously, and the real thrill of con-valescence coincided with the moment when I could kneel up and survey for myself once more every detail of my 'manor' of St Leonard's Road, Ullin, Teviot and Dewberry Streets from those all-embracing windows!

My mother, I imagine, must have given serious thought to the problem of my healthy development. Fresh air was the crying need and suitable playgrounds the real crux of the matter, especially in a hot, dry summer when the stale breeze stirred idly above the pavements and the fried fish shop fat smelt worse than usual; and not only for the 'parson's kids' but for all the children of the parish who had nowhere to play but the streets, nothing to play with but the lamp-posts and the area railings, nothing to sit on in the open air save the front-doorstep of their homes or the kerbstones. And there they would sit in rows, the tiny ones, the toddlers who could not manage to go far afield, their feet in the refuse of the gutters, the filth from the road blowing in their faces.

So haunted were my parents by this tragic lack that they tried to raise enough money from their friends to buy a small timber-yard, out of which they hoped to make some sort of playground; but its astute owner, scenting an uncommercial venture, put up the price and they could not find the necessary sum. The older children were capable of walking or riding— unlawfully, by hanging to the backs of wagons—as far as Victoria Park, traditional recreation-ground of Cockneys. Even so, it was some distance to the north of us in Hackney; out of the question for Nanny and myself save as a full-dress expedition in a horse-drawn cab. Then there were the church-yards, such as that of St Anne's, Limehouse, as large as a small park—it had been larger before they cut off a corner to

make the Commercial Road—and beautifully tended with
wide green lawns and well-kept flowerbeds; but a child does
not care to play among gravestones. The Island Gardens, oasis
of foliage in a desert of buildings at the southern extremity
of the Isle of Dogs, were nearly as distant as Victoria Park
and liable, moreover, to be cut off for hours at a time by the
swing-bridges giving access to the Millwall Basins. The
Tunnel Gardens were no more than a narrow strip of shrubs
and flowers squeezed alongside the entrance to the Blackwall
Tunnel, where old people sunned themselves on rows of
benches—which were also a popular resort of fleas—sheltered
from the east wind by the high brick wall of the Docks.

The Docks! They supplied an answer to the problem that,
like all brilliant solutions, was simplicity itself. Almost on
our doorstep lay the finest playground of all, safe, free from
crowds, as airy as you could wish, open, in fact, to the four
winds of heaven and the salt sea breeze borne in from the
lower reaches of the River on the swelling crest of each flood-
tide. My father—it must have been his idea—knew someone
who carried the requisite amount of weight in Port of London
Authority circles, and a permanent pass to the East India
Dock was made out in the name of Nanny, myself, and even,
to begin with, mentioning the pram! I never set eyes on this
famous document; indeed, I doubt if we ever carried it about
with us. In any case, the child, the nurse, and the pram
became well-known enough to the police on duty at the Dock
gate, that handsome, classic gateway designed by Rennie,
with the wide central arch for vehicles flanked by two narrow
arches for pedestrians, through which the easterly gales in
winter-time would whistle with such force that we could
hardly make our way against them. I must have seen this
gateway almost daily during the nine years that we lived in
Poplar, and its shape, proportions, design and colouring
remained stamped with perfect clarity upon my visual memory
from the leaded roof of the clock-tower, or turret, by which

it was surmounted, to the massive granite blocks at its base, from which the iron-rimmed wheels of the drays drew sparks as they struck them a grating blow in passing. I was not to see it again for a quarter of a century; then it was as familiar still in every line as though barely a week had gone by since last I had set eyes on it.

That solid portal only rarely presented to the outside world the spectacle of its huge, studded wooden doors closed and barred, on such occasions, if I remember rightly, as Good Friday and Christmas Day. Once within that adventurous region, a whole vista of strange and thrilling sights would unfold; not a week went by without a visit, and in fine weather we went there almost every day.

The East India Dock was busy enough in that first decade of the century when a ship of 6,000 tons was considered large, and one of 12,000 tons would have been described as an 'ocean giant'. The true 'giants' of that epoch were to be found further downstream at Woolwich and Tilbury—just as today the largest P. & O. and Orient ships loom, vast as cathedrals, above the Essex marshes; but a great mass of shipping was then of a size to use the East India Dock with comfort. The majority were cargo-vessels, although every Friday—a day of excitement not to be missed on any account—the Batavier Line ships sailed with passengers from the Blackwall Pier. I have no idea how far they were going, but from the scenes which took place at the moment of embarkation you would have imagined them to be sailing to the ends of the earth never to return, such were the farewells, the tears and lamentations, the cries and groans and frantic wavings as the ship moved out into the stream.

In my own mind I decided that they were emigrating to Australia, a place already firmly established in my consciousness as the furthest possible point from England on the surface of the globe, only to be reached, otherwise than by a ship, through the doubtful expedient of falling through the manholes in the street: was I not carefully warned by Nanny always to avoid them, if I did not wish to find myself turning up in Australia, condemned for ever to walk upside down? In all probability, however, the Batavier Line was transporting them no further than Rotterdam.

I fancy, too, that the Union-Castle Intermediates took on passengers at Blackwall; certainly those unique, lavender-coloured hulls, combination of genius with the white super-structure and vermilion, black-topped funnels, are amongst my earliest recollections in the world of ships. Few vessels were more distinctive or more calculated to impress the memory, for there were not such a number of different colourings or funnel-designs as there are today. The sea enjoyed a monopoly of the means of transport between conti-nents, and shipping companies basked in the sunshine of comparative security. There was less foreign competition, and since Blériot had not yet flown the Channel, no one yet dreamed of a serious challenge from the air. Passengers did not demand extremes of luxury and entertainment. Content to be reasonably well-victualled and bedded with a fair degree of comfort, they were still sufficiently well pleased to arrive safely at their journey's end, although shipwrecks were rapidly becoming scarce.

Shipowners might vye with one another in matters of size and speed, but they did not find it necessary to compete in producing revolutionary colour-schemes or ultra-modern designs conceived with one eye on the cruise-enthusiast and the round-voyage traveller. Plain, sensible black for funnels and hull, with brown or white for the upperworks was a very common colouring: dingy enough, unless streaked with rust or daubed with scarlet patches of red lead.

I was not entirely ignorant of ships. They were discussed quite often in my hearing, for my grandfather made propellers for some of the largest vessels afloat—for warships, too—so that when I sang, to my father's accompaniment on the study piano, Kipling's 'Riddle' from the *Just So Song Book*, I had more than an inkling of what I was singing about.

> 'China-going P. and O.'s
> Pass Pau Amma's playground close',

I would warble lustily, although at that stage I doubt whether I should have taken much notice of a sombre P. and O. in her unique black-and-stone colour paint, if I had seen one in the River. But I wished heartily that those famous sister-ships of the Royal Mail Line, the *Don* and the *Magdalena*, would sail from London instead of Southampton, so that I might see for myself the 'great steamers white and gold' that went 'rolling down to Rio'.

Unfortunately, the better-known passenger-ships—with the exception of Union Castle—did not come so far up the River as the Blackwall Reach. The Union Castle, of course, I thought magnificent; the others hardly less so; but the ships that I admired in childhood would look decidedly odd today, if any of them are still in existence, with their immensely tall, thin funnels, either bolt upright or heavily raked; straight stems; hulls without sheer and superstructures innocent of streamlining. Most noticeable of all, perhaps, would be their lofty masts still crossed by a substantial yard from which, if the need to set a topsail on it had long disappeared, mail-pennants and signal-flags could at least be flown conspicuously and with some dignity. But then I am old-fashioned enough to consider that the modern mastless ship, for all its prac-ticability and economy, looks unnaturally truncated like a badly pollarded tree; and the jumble of house-flags, courtesy-flags, signals and pennants crowded together on the stump-pole which passes as an apology for a mast is merely confusing and faintly ridiculous.

As fascinating as the ships themselves—and far more interesting to a child than the passengers—were the cargoes. I have never forgotten the unloading of a whole shipload of wild animals destined for the Zoo. Like most London children I visited the Zoo regularly and with enjoyment; but this was a very different matter to the spectacle of bored creatures pacing their cages or dozing in a corner. For hours my father and I watched enthralled while lions, leopards, and a puma—most savage of all—were hoisted from the deck into the air, spitting and choking with rage at the indignities they were forced to endure as the cages slipped and lurched in the slings, and the fear they were compelled to feel at this horrible new experience.

There were dangerous snakes as well, but they were less spectacular, being mercifully comatose and clearly unwilling to escape. The mate of the ship allowed us to peer between the splines of a crate at the monstrous, heaving coils of a python or boa-constrictor—I have forgotten which; I noted with a sick fascination the large bulge that represented its dinner.

Cargoes were discharged in bulk more frequently than they are nowadays and lay in great heaps about the wharves. There was something peculiarly enjoyable about running up the steep side of a pyramid of maize or brown sugar until your feet sank in too far and the stuff got into your shoes. Hygienic standards of the time were low; it never occurred to me that this was not very nice for the people who were going to eat the sugar, any more than it did to the stevedores who shovelled it up from the wet surface of the wharf. After all, as a generation we were brought up to dispel fastidiousness with the belief that we must all eat a peck of dirt before we die! I saw no reason to doubt this oft-repeated saying; but I should have been a good deal happier if I had known exactly how large a peck of dirt could be.

Nanny and I would confine ourselves to a sedate promenade of the quays, admiring the ships and watching the cargo-work from a safe distance; but as I grew older there were certain red letter days when my father took me to the docks. For much of his parish visiting he used a big green bicycle, specially strengthened to support his weight; just as soon as I was grown enough and sensible enough to sit fair and square astride the carrier of this splendid machine, we would ride together to the River.

'Hold on to me—tight!' he would command, when I had clambered a little uncertainly into position. My arms were too short to reach round his middle, but I would grasp the pocket-flaps of his jacket, and away we would go, with scarcely a wobble, down St Leonard's Road.

It was a wonderful way of getting along: all the smoothness of an engineless progression and none of the hard work of pedalling. I had nothing to do but hang on and look about me to my heart's content, except that I could not see ahead for the vast barrier of my father's back. Approaching the junction with the East India Dock Road, I would grow apprehensive, although the traffic, being mostly horse-drawn, was really no match for a bicycle.

'Keep still—don't wriggle!' thundered my father as in my anxiety I tried to see round him. There was a nervous moment or two as we crossed the stream of traffic, while a tram-driver rang his bell peremptorily at us and a cart-horse breathed heavily in the region of my neck; then we were safely under the archway of the Dock entrance.

In my father's company anything might happen; the afternoon would be one long sequence of adventures. We might be invited to mount the footplate of a shunting-engine, or to climb a spidery ladder to the driving-cab of a crane. I nursed a secret suspicion towards these cranes, ever since one had startled me nearly out of my wits by moving suddenly towards me along the rails upon which its wheeled feet rested. My father's chuckles, and the sight of the grinning crane-driver overhead—with whom, of course, he had been in collusion— neither salved my wounded pride at being made to look foolish—children, like dogs, hate to be laughed at—nor weakened my belief, which lasted for a considerable time, in the ability of cranes to move on their own.

Sometimes we were invited on board ships, for my father was the sort of genial and friendly person with whom all sorts and conditions of men felt instantly at ease; and for a landsman, he could talk with sense and authority about seafaring matters. In small, dark, and fusty cabins we would be given cups of tea—strong, with condensed milk, very preferable to the watered-down nursery variety. We would be shown over bridges, which I liked, although there was little to inspect save the wheel and the binnacle and I was too short to see over the dodger. We would be shown over engine-rooms as well, which I detested, being consumed with a paralysing fear from the moment I set foot on the iron ladder leading to the noisy, hot, sulphurous cavern below until I stepped out of the engine-room fiddley into the light of day once more. Nor have I ever lost my dislike of wisps of steam, and the incredibly bright eye of furnaces, and moving masses of well-polished, well-greased machinery which I still distrust and still do not even wish to understand.

Even more alarming would be our descent into the bottom of a dry-dock, where the oppressive bulk of the ship's hull loomed terrifyingly above our heads. I kept very close to my father's side down there. Not for worlds would I have admitted the intense relief with which we began to climb the long flight of slimy stone steps that led us back to ground-level! Not only was I afraid of the ship falling off the chocks and crushing us, but another hazard threatened in the shape of ominous gouts of water spurting through the cracks and hinges of the dock-gate caissons far above our heads. It seemed to me that at any moment the weight of the river outside would burst through and overwhelm us in a Niagara of water. There was also that little quirk of fear experienced whenever we crossed the narrow gates of a lock, fenced in by nothing more than loosely-hung, thin iron chains. My head for heights was good enough, and I had no hesitation in looking down at the brown water lapping below us at the wooden doors; but just as we stepped from one gate to the next, I would feel a momentary panic dread that they would begin to open, leaving me with a foot on each.

Dry-dock visiting left me with a permanent affection for the smell of 'compo', the reddish-brown anti-fouling composition with which ships' bottoms are painted after cleaning. To Nanny's disgust I would usually return from this sort of expedition with the stuff on my shoes or clothes, and I would be secretly delighted if I had brought home a little of the smell as well.

Many square-rigged ships still used the East India Dock, and my father, passionately addicted to small-boat sailing, was drawn to them as by a magnet. Over most things I followed his likes and dislikes with slavish devotion, but in this case I hardly shared his enthusiasm. I could see that they were far more beautiful than the unlovely steamships of the day; but sailing-ships inspired in me a kind of nameless apprehension: to me they all seemed doomed. I called them, stubbornly, by the private name of 'storm-ships', and no amount of adult persuasion could extract from me its derivation nor make me give up using it. I can only conclude that I had read so many books about sailing-ships by Marryat, Henty, Bullen, and above all, Clark Russell—*The Wreck of the 'Grosvenor'* was an early favourite—in which voyage after voyage ended disastrously in strandings, founderings, dismastings, mutinies and other marine catastrophes, that I became convinced of the extreme improbability of any sailing-ship ever reaching her destination.

A possible influence of more personal application was the story of my Great-uncle Reginald, the only professional sea-faring man in our family, who had been a mate in sail. He was reputed to have served at some time in his career in the renowned *Sobraon*; and a painting of this great ship listed over in a heavy gale, surrounded by huge seas, her black-and-white chequered side illuminated by a single shaft of wintry light, hung in my grandparents' house. I admired it greatly, but it did nothing to further my confidence in the stability of the sailing-ship. Great-uncle Reginald was my grandmother's favourite brother, and a close bond of affection existed between them. One night my grandmother awoke to see her brother standing at the foot of the bed, dressed in sou'-wester and oilskins. He called her urgently: 'Fanny! Fanny!' She heard his voice plainly, but as from far away; and she saw with horror that water dripped from his clothes. The streaming figure raised its arms despairingly and vanished, leaving my grandmother with the conviction that she had not dreamed a dream but experienced a supernatural visitation, although she had no previous tendency to second sight. As sensible and practical as she was clever, she woke up my grandfather and told him what had happened. Together they noted the time; and later it was discovered to have been almost the moment when, his ship having gybed all-standing in heavy weather, Great-uncle Reginald had been swept off the poop by the spanker-boom, not to be seen again.

The omens, then, for me were unfavourable to sailing-ships; and while my father endeavoured to familiarise me with the correct names of yards, sails and rigging, I was far more interested in the livestock forward of the main-mast. There were so many halyards, downhauls, clew-lines and bunt-lines to remember, the masts were so tall and the web of standing and running parts so intricate, although I dare say the ships I knew were 'bald-headed' enough by then in comparison to their prosperous days. Already the steamers had captured the cream of any trade, and sail was being skimped and starved and forced downhill to ultimate extinction. Like any object that is out-moded but still in use, to us they were just 'old-fashioned', all but finished with and futureless. Only when they were on the point of disappearance did sailing-ships acquire a sudden glamour, so that people talk today of the 'romance of sail', treasuring every scrap of knowledge and recollection with a pious care. I should, I feel, be able to remember more clearly what those sailing-ships were like. Yet, I am ashamed to say, my only truthful, vivid memory is of a pig, plump, pink and very clean, by whose pen, situated comfortably abaft a small deckhouse, I spent an absorbing afternoon while my father held a long conversation with the mate. They came forward eventually to find out what I was up to.

'Ah, that pig, now,' said the mate. 'Fine fellow, isn't he? We shall get some good dinners off him!'

I could hardly believe my ears. But it was true enough. He would be killed and eaten, the mate assured us, long before they reached Cape Leeuwin: somewhere in the South Atlantic, he would say. The thought of this abominable fate overhanging the pig, now happily grunting in his pen, was overwhelming. I began to cry, and had to be led hastily to the cuddy, where tea and biscuits were produced in an attempt to erase the bad impression made by the destiny of the pig. And further to distract my mind from this unfortunate episode, the mate —he had heavy moustaches—showed me, with sympathetic care, something I had certainly not seen before: the brass lamp hanging in gimbals above the cuddy-table which would remain at precisely the same level however violently the ship might roll.

It seems to me that in those long and happy afternoons we must have wandered far and wide along the banks of the Thames. We visited other docks occasionally, although I have no notion how we got from one to the other; explored the labyrinths of Millwall and West India, even the distant Surrey Commercial across the River, with such romantically named basins as Lavender, Lady, Russia and Stave, where the neat stacks of timber gave out aromatic smells in the sunshine; and at some time during the year 1910 I was taken to see over Captain Scott's ship the *Terra Nova*, fitting out in St Katharine's for her ill-fated voyage to the Antarctic. She seemed small enough, even to a seven-year-old child, for that tremendous task, as she lay in a corner of the basin overshadowed by the bleak façades of grimy warehouses. My mother had brought some of the famous Nelson 'red seven-pennies' to tuck into an odd bookshelf, hoping that they might help to dispel a few hours of boredom; and I myself was deterred reluctantly from ramming a bag of sticky sweets down behind the cushions of a settee. The expedition had engaged my interest so that I prayed with all my might that Captain Scott should be the first person to reach the South Pole; we saw nothing in the least shameful then in wishing for honours, glory and aggrandisement for our own country.

But the East India was *our* dock, the one I knew—and therefore liked—the best, stubbornly defending it against all others, despite its smallness, with a fierce proprietary partiality. After all, the dock never failed me; never once did it lack some reward for going there, like a benevolent uncle who provides a tip at every visit. Perhaps it would be nothing more than the spicy scents issuing from the godowns, the piles of mysterious sacks and bales containing some unimaginable commodity, strange barks, gums or roots from which came those wonderful smells, acrid or sweet, which seemed to me the very essence of those 'foreign parts' about which I read with such assiduity in a small, old, blue-covered book called *Uncle Ned's Stories of the Tropics*.

Sometimes there would be a diver to watch as he ponderously went down his little ladder into the water until his round, shiny helmet had disappeared beneath the surface and the bursting bubbles alone revealed where he stalked, a monstrous figure, about the dock-bottom; or a coffer-dam in course of construction when a dock-gate had to be renewed. Best of all, in hot, fine weather, we would set off at once for the Brunswick Wharf, there to spend hours enthralled by the ships as they hurried up Bugsby's Reach on the full of the flood—'a penny if you can read her name before I do!'—and the fascinating spectacle, then so common, of Thames barges, handled by experts, manœuvring in that crowded tideway. Many an object lesson did my father demonstrate through the agency of those master-helmsmen, the barge-skippers. Even my undeveloped and untutored discrimination could detect the perfect blend of experience and skill with which they used the tide in mid-stream or the slack water inshore, and the wind working with, and at times against, the tide, to send and to place their craft exactly as they wished. Even I could perceive the niceties of their judgement in taking the way off a barge, perhaps loaded to her gunwales, by choosing the precise moment at which to lower a headsail or brail up the main.

I could not imagine a more agreeable manner in which to pass the afternoon. There, on the very brink of the stream, we were free of the stale, dry, dusty heat of the land. The wide Thames sparkled in the sun, the wavelets slapped the wharf with a refreshing sound, the cool smell of water and mud rose to our noses. There was an exhilarating sense of movement, of the whole great tideway flowing past us up to London or ebbing down-river to the sea itself.

It must have been here that I made two discoveries of great importance: the tremendous charm exercised by water, even the turbid water of the Thames, moving or still, whipped into a small, choppy sea or calm as a mirror in the sheltered dock; and the unrivalled fascination of a ship's bow—of any bow, whether boat or barge, steam or sail—cleaving through that water.

In the docks themselves I learned other things as well: to skip out of the way of the cranes that straddled the quay when they began to move along on their iron legs; to 'stand from under' when a sling of cargo was swinging overhead—although no one could have been more considerate of one's safety than the average London stevedore; to look warily as I passed the open doors of any godown, in case a heavy truck of goods was coming out; and to keep well clear of bollards on the quayside when a ship was making fast or casting off.

Most fortunate of all, I acquired an early familiarity with ships, and tides, with tugs and barges, locks and lighters. I became accustomed at this tender age to the idea of ships arriving with cargoes from all parts of the world, discharging, loading, and sailing again. This simple rotation of a seaman's duties impressed itself upon my mind with the obviousness of an every-day fact, as a country child notes the inevitability of harvest following on seed-time, reaping upon sowing.

Had I but known it, I was beginning an education that was to be of incalculable help and value to me in my adult life.

4. The Penitent Bargee

NOT unnaturally, as the child of a parson, the Church occupied a prominent position in my life. Physically, its presence was close and real; the large bulk of it towered protectively above our house and garden; its bell ringing for service marked our days; on warm summer Sundays the sound of lusty hymn-singing filtered through its open windows. Spiritually, like most children of my kind and generation, I had the advantage of an early introduction to its mode of life and standard of behaviour, was instructed in its precepts, taught to repeat my prayers and Catechism, to learn the Collects and to read the Bible, while I cannot even remember when I first began to go to church on Sunday mornings.

To start with I was allowed to stay until the sermon; or perhaps it would be more exactly truthful to say that I was allowed to *leave* at that point, my sister and I scuttling out hand in hand with a somewhat undignified haste in the brief interval after the Creed—our principal service being the Sung Eucharist. Later we were considered capable of sitting through the sermon itself: an excellent arrangement while my sister was still at home, for it enabled us to emerge from the ordeal of keeping quiet and behaving as the little Vicarage children should before our self-discipline had begun to wear thin. To be fidgety or talkative in church was, we knew, as disrespectful as it would have been in Buckingham Palace. Modern children seem to be allowed to chat, sing, hum, crawl about the pews and generally distract the attention and disturb the devotions of members of the congregation, while their parents exchange above their heads gratified smiles at such demonstrations of individuality by their young. One is obliged to conclude either that they have not been made to understand what the church is for or why they are there, or that no one has attempted to teach them the rudiments of self-control.

When my sister left for boarding-school, a new and appalling consequence loomed unexpectedly upon my otherwise unclouded horizon: I was pronounced of an age, and sufficiently responsible, to take myself home from church. It was no distance, and nothing of an ordeal. I merely had to turn left outside the west door of the church, follow round the high wooden fence of the Vicarage until I came to our gate, open it, and I was home. In that, of course, lay one of the more alarming possibilities. Our gates, of solid wood, had to be fastened by Yale locks in order to discourage, although not to prevent, the local populace from slipping inside and using the meagre shelter of our privet bushes as a public convenience. These gates were no more than chest-high to the average adult; in other words, it was simplicity itself to put an arm over and unlatch the lock. But to me, at full stretch and on tiptoe, it was a physical impossibility to touch the top, let alone to reach the catch. For some reason, not apparent to me at this distance of time, this lock could not be fastened back; and as we set out for church, it was my special care to see that my mother had put a large stone between the gates to prevent them slamming to and shutting me out. How

I fussed about those stones! All through the service the horrid
thought kept obtruding itself, worrying and nagging, like a
thorn in the finger or a fish-bone in one's throat: had the gate
slammed to? And if it had, how was I to get in?

And this was by no means the only distraction, for the
whole business filled me with unreasoning terror; I discovered that one of the most hateful eventualities in the world
consisted in having to do something by oneself! The sermon
finished, we rose for the offertory hymn, my collection-penny
gripped despairingly in a sticky palm. Once it had been
dropped into the sidesman's little bag, there was no going
back. My mother's hand propelled me gently towards the
aisle. Normally a tremendous ritualist, I enjoyed bowing to
the altar, but now it became a mere perfunctory bob. I was
out of the pew, alone in the vast wastes of the middle aisle,
which appeared to elongate itself into an endless vista with
the west door as an impossibly distant haven. (Perhaps this
is one of the reasons why, since attaining independence, I have
always preferred to sit at the very back of the church.) My
trembling legs could not carry me fast enough between the
serried ranks of the congregation, all, it seemed, staring at
me with curious or accusing eyes, as much as to say: 'So *that*
little girl can't last the service out!' In reality, of course, they
scarcely gave a passing glance to the Vicar's younger daughter,
in button boots and bonnet, scuttering out of church like a
terrified rabbit.

Once outside, the worst was still to come. Clutching desperately my prayer-book and Hymns A. & M., with thumping heart I traversed the enormous stretch of pavement until
I came at last to the fatal gate. The relief when I had got
inside was immense. No early settler pursued to the very
walls of a frontier fort by Red Indians could have felt a
greater sense of deliverance from peril as the gates of the
stockade closed fast behind him. Now I had only to run up
the front-door steps and ring the bell. On alternate Sundays

Nanny would be out, attending the neighbouring church of St Frideswide's—for she preferred not to be a member of her employer's congregation—but either Elizabeth, the house-parlourmaid, or Mrs Packer, the cook, would be there to let me in. The footsteps in answer to my ring were sometimes slow in coming, and my imagination would begin to paint a panic-stricken picture of a deserted house. They had gone out —had run away—had even dropped down dead. Then the door would open, and the ordeal by solitude would be over for another week.

There was at least one agonising occasion, a Sunday of high winds, when the gate had blown shut. I knew the worst as soon as I rounded the corner and saw the very stone with which we had sought to keep the gates ajar lying right out on the pavement. I pushed with all my might, but unavailingly: the gate was firmly fastened. I stood helpless and completely at a loss. Being Sunday, there was scarcely anyone about: a few men, in their best caps, making for the public-houses; a child emerging from the Bottle and Jug, carrying carefully home the Sunday-dinner beer. None of them showed the slightest interest in me standing outside the Vicarage gate, and I was not at all sure that I wanted them to do so. How desperately I longed to see my mother's familiar figure in her plain, dark coat and rather shabby hat; but half an hour or more must pass before she could possibly appear, and half an hour is a very long time to spend loitering outside your own front-gate, while passers-by stare and wonder what you are doing there. Like all who are unsure of themselves, and especially the very young, I hated to be conspicuous.

As the final touch of disaster, it began to rain. My Sunday coat and bonnet would be spoiled and Nanny would be vexed; I should get wet, I should catch cold, perhaps develop bronchitis—I might even die! The pathos of my situation became too much for me and I burst into tears, sobbing with self-pity at the idea of being shut out of my own home while

Mother and Nanny sang hymns unconcernedly in their respective churches, Mrs Packer cooked our Sunday luncheon, and Elizabeth relaxed unheeding with her family in nearby Bow.

'What's the matter, young lady? Got locked out?'

It was the police-constable on his beat who finally rescued me. I suppose I thanked him—I sincerely hope so; I can only remember explaining my dilemma and bolting through the gate, once he had opened it, with an unbounded sense of relief and gratitude.

The church of St Michael and All Angels had dignity in the height and sweep of the chancel arch, and its proportions could be considered noble in any other medium but the yellow brick said to be particularly fancied by the East Londoner, especially in conjunction with a slated roof. Indeed, its sole interior structural decoration consisted of brickwork, in red and black bands or diamond patterns, a form of ornamentation exploited to the utmost by the economical nineteenth-century architect to outline the arches and windows, or to break up the terrible monotony of a lofty wall. I have read that there is much solid worth about this copious Victorian use of brickwork; nevertheless such utilitarian and dreary material, more suitable to the construction of schools, factories, or railway stations, seemed hardly worth the ingenuity and labour lavished on it when the result was merely uninspiring.

St Michael's could boast little stonework; plenty of pitchpine in pews and roof; indifferent stained glass; a low, sparse, metal screen; a wooden pulpit well, if plainly, carved; and a massive brass lectern cast in the conventional style of an eagle with outspread wings, but a singularly plump eagle with the most imperious eye, a ferocious beak, and tremendous claws clutching a large brass globe in their relentless grip. This eagle alone must have used up an inordinate amount of metal-polish and energy in its weekly Saturday cleaning. I admired it enormously; and since the Vicarage pew happened to be on the same side, I could spend long, agreeable periods noting

73

its attractions with an appreciative eye. But then I thought the whole church magnificent—was it not my father's church? —and St Michael himself the most auspicious and powerful of patron saints under whose protection we were fortunate to dwell—let alone all his attendant angels, who ought surely to come in useful at some time or another during 'the changes and chances of this mortal life'? At least, I liked to think that we had a slight priority claim on their vigilance when we were crossing the East India Dock Road, or going through the Blackwall Tunnel, or sailing in mid-Channel on our summer holidays; and I felt almost sorry for Nanny, who only had someone rather ineffectual like St Frideswide, an Abbess, to call upon in time of trouble.

Certainly, on high festivals, with flowers upon the altar and all the candles lit, banners embroidered in rich reds, blues and golds brought out in readiness for a procession, and the large congregation singing some well-known hymn with simple vigour, our church, transformed into a place of warmth and colour, positively glowed with fervour and good fellowship.

Just as the captain's personality can permeate the atmosphere of the largest ship, so the incumbent's nature must inevitably affect the whole spiritual condition of his parish; if my father's church was well-attended, his strength of character and genial presence were responsible to no small extent. It was the day of giants in the East End parishes: priests of the calibre of Father Wainwright and Father Dolling, whose names were commonly on people's lips. My father did not attain this higher category, but at least he inspired a trustful confidence from which faith and affection grew, and he built up a parish organisation in the face of difficulties that would have wearied or broken a weaker spirit. His parish, although small in actual area, was densely over-populated. Today, following the widespread destruction of two wars, and thanks to better housing conditions, 12,000 people occupy a space where close on 30,000 were then obliged to live. The visiting alone in such a district was a formidable task. There was always money to be raised: endless sums were needed for repairs to the church, for food, clothing and medicines for the destitute, for the building of the parish hall and its proper maintenance, such a centre being of vital importance in such a district. With the best will in the world, the congregations themselves were quite unable to support their church; the collections were pitifully small. You could not ask these people for new vestments or hangings for the church when they had little enough to spare for their own clothing or the adequate furnishing of their homes; and my father would augment such diocesan funds as might be available by preaching at wealthy churches in the West End of London—such as his old parish of Lancaster Gate—and the rich holiday resorts of the South Coast. It was an unashamed wringing of the Belgravian withers, a harrowing of the tender Bournemouth hearts; but he would bring home on Sunday nights a small leather bag stuffed with notes, gold and silver to the tune of several hundred pounds, and the end, he considered, had more than justified the means.

In the daily practice of his religion he was what is called today an Anglo-Catholic, but at that time was more commonly known as 'High Church'. The ritual, with the colour and music which it introduced into the conduct of services, appealed considerably to his parishioners, possibly because their own lives and surroundings were so totally devoid of either. But he abhorred above all things that product of ritualism then known as a 'spike': the kind of mentality that attributed a higher importance to the outward ceremony than to its inward significance. He believed that the Church, in the accumulated wisdom of her long survival, had fittingly ordained these things in the knowledge that they helped the ordinary, fallible 'inward eye of faith' to see, and enter more fully into the inner mysteries. Beyond that, and the promotion of a proper seemliness and reverence in the services, ceremony had no meaning for him.

Naturally enough, the average East Ender knew little or nothing of such matters, and his abysmal ignorance provoked many incidents of unconscious humour. On Good Fridays the neighbouring parishes combined with ours to hold a Procession of Witness through the streets, usually with the Bishop of Stepney—if one may say so without disrespect—as the principal attraction. At the nursery window I would watch for its appearance from the direction of the East India Dock Road. It was an impressive spectacle. The street, empty of its normal traffic, would fill rapidly as the sound of distant hymn-singing brought people running from their houses to line the pavements. At the end of St Leonard's Road would appear the head of the procession, a huge, plain, red wooden cross held high above the marchers. The advancing banners swayed, choir surplices fluttered, the brass of band instruments glittered in the spring sunshine. As the serried ranks of the faithful drew level with the Vicarage, I looked eagerly for my father, wearing his vestments with his usual dignity, for my mother walking sedately with the Women's Guild, and for the Bishop himself, adequately imposing in his purple cope, his mitre on his head, his pastoral staff in his hand. People poured out of the pubs to see what all the noise and singing was about; and suddenly confronted with this bewildering sight, the bystanders reacted with the typical outspoken comments of the Cockney.

'Cor! Look, Bill, 'ere's a chap wearing an 'earthrug!'

'Strewth! Look at the ole bloke in the crocodile 'at!'

'Crocodile 'at? That's the bleedin' tea-cosy!'

My mother's composure was once badly shaken when, walking nearest to the pavement, she heard a dismayed voice remarking: 'All the ugly old women in Poplar out for a walk!' 'It was so hard not to laugh!' she confessed later.

What ultimate impression such demonstrations made on

the fuddled minds of the onlookers it is difficult to tell; at least they bore witness, as they were designed to do, to the origin of Good Friday as something quite opposed to the secular idea of just another holiday to be spent either in the 'boozer' or kicking a football aimlessly about a piece of waste-ground.

With the marchers themselves the Good Friday Procession grew in popularity. It was a concrete manifestation of faith highly approved of by the East Ender, who did not understand or hold with any blurred edges to his Christianity: a practical opportunity to show to all the world on which side of the line he chose to stand. One year the members of the Womens' Guild waiting at the assembly point were perturbed to see a body of men approaching determinedly from the direction of Bethnal Green, a place noted for its roughs. Their leader ranged his followers on either side of the women's section, and then explained with cheerful confidence that they had heard there might be 'trouble'; their Vicar had sent them to 'look after' anyone who might be disposed to make it.

Until the end of his days my father would uphold his firm conviction that his East End parishioners—of whom he spoke invariably with nostalgic affection—made the most wholehearted of Christians, once they had decided upon a change of course. Half-and-half measures did not appeal; there was no 'Sundays Only' Christianity in Poplar; it was all or nothing; and as an illustration he loved to tell the story of the penitent bargee.

This man, tough and brawny, his bullet-head covered with ginger-coloured hair, stubbly save in front where it was oiled and trained into a luxuriant quiff, his blue eyes fiery with drink and the weather of a score of Thames-side winters, had a shocking reputation as a foul-mouthed drunkard and a wife-beater into the bargain. But somewhere among the mean streets of Poplar he found his road leading to Damascus, repented of his sins, amended his ways, and became the most

77

ardent of Christians. He gave up swearing and drinking; he began to treat his wife as a human being. He was baptised and later confirmed after a careful preparation by my father. There was no more assiduous church-goer in the parish; he even acquired the habit of reciting the Angelus at the prescribed hours of six o'clock in the morning, noon, and six o'clock at night. No matter that the appointed moment caught him on the deck of his barge, in the very act of clearing the gates of a lock or picking up a line from a tug. First things first: down would go his long sweep, and the devout bargee would remain standing motionless, head bent, while he repeated to himself the versicles and responses of the Angelus, and the traffic of the Thames could, for all he cared, go to blazes. In vain the tug-skippers and lock-masters poured down upon his bowed head a flow of abuse such as he could have equalled formerly but now denied himself, while his barge drifted unchecked upon the tideway. Not until the final 'Amen' had been pronounced did he pick up his sweep and get his lighter under control once more.

After a probationary period with scarcely a backsliding, he became a server at St Michael's; and my father having introduced the use of incense into the principal services, the reformed drunkard reached his apotheosis as a thurifer. He performed his duties with great dignity: the scarlet cassock and lace-edged cotter became him surprisingly well, if the colour clashed a little with the ginger quiff and the purplish complexion, glowing now with conscious pride where previously it had glowed with beer. The ginger moustache bristled with rectitude; and the large, clumsy hands, calloused and thickened with the constant use of wood and iron, and now encased in an enormous pair of white cotton gloves, manipulated the thin brass chains of the censer with loving delicacy and care.

There was something specially disarming about his sincerity, his simple, rock-like faith, immovable as mountains and burning with a warm clarity. He was one of the first-fruits of my father's sowing in that arid soil; the harvest must long be reaped by now, and that trusting soul, secure in the certitude of his beliefs, has been safely gathered in.

My father always stressed the prime importance of getting the menfolk of the parish to come to church; he used to say that a congregation composed almost entirely of women denoted a parson who had failed in his job. On Sunday afternoons he held a special service for men. The hearty roar of their voices bawling out the more martial hymn-tunes would reach me in the Vicarage garden in summer-time, or even in the nursery where I sat at my painting or drawing, wishing earnestly that Nanny's 'Sunday off' would come to an end; and the congregation streaming out of church in their best suits, clean white chokers and tidy caps was a signal that the long, quiet afternoon was nearly over.

Although my father always took this service himself, he would invite anyone he thought suitable to speak to the men, and one of these visiting preachers was George Lansbury. I personally never saw Lansbury, but he made a great impression on my parents. Already he was famous in Poplar for his unremitting championship of the working-man, but from my angle he belonged in that obscure adult region known as politics, then far above my head. There was, I knew, someone very contemptible called Lloyd George, who caused my father to rattle angrily the pages of *The Times* or the *Standard* and exclaim: 'Dreadful little Welsh nonconformist!' And I had heard him say that 'the Conservatives, after all, are the best of a bad bunch', although I never discovered of *what* bunch he was talking. Yet my father, the lifelong, if sometimes disapproving Tory, and Lansbury the passionate Socialist, saw eye-to-eye on many matters, for Lansbury was also a deeply religious man.

His address to the men was memorable. He spoke to them of their 'duty towards their neighbour'; how imperative it was that each should do all in his power to help those worse off than themselves; they were not to be content because they had a comparatively secure and decently paid job. Then he reminded them that there existed also their 'duty towards God'; that they must never forget Him nor turn their backs upon Him; if ever they did so, he warned them, their greatest material gain would be as so much dust and ashes for all the happiness it would bring them. After the service, he came to the Vicarage for a cup of tea; and my mother, no less than my father, realised that she had made the acquaintance of a most remarkable man, the very antithesis of those Socialist leaders of today who have no other yardstick but money and power. How he would have despised the attitude of mind embodied in the phrase 'what's in it for me?'; and castigated those trade union officials who use the backs of the workers as stepping stones to their own personal affluence!

One of the most flourishing men's organisations connected with our church was St Michael's Brass Band, in which my father played either the cornet or the French horn as necessity dictated: a versatility prompted, I imagine, more by a desire to encourage the others than by any special aptitude for brass, his favourite instrument being the 'cello. The band was much in demand on all sorts of occasions such as the Good Friday procession, carol-singing at Christmas, outdoor mission services and various functions in the Parish Hall. Brass bands were then as popular as they still are in the northern half of England; many churches and chapels, and most active bodies possessed their own. The Salvation Army in particular paraded in full strength on Sundays, holding skirmishes with Satan at every promising street-corner. Unfortunately, whether through accident or design, they chose to mount an especially powerful attack on the forces of evil just outside St Michael's during morning service, accompanied by a band in which the fervour of the performance outweighed a certain lack of ear in the performers.

No one acknowledged more sincerely than my father the good work done by the Salvationists, but he really could not put up with this penetrating cacophony which drowned his sermons, and, on occasion, the most solemn parts of the Liturgy. For it happened more than once; the sidesmen or a churchwarden would go out and reason with the skirmishers, requesting them to move to some other part of the battle-front; but eventually my father had to make representations to the local headquarters.

Doubtless the worthy Salvationists, intent on their own form of worship, could not realise how seriously they were interfering with ours. At least, that is the construction I like to place upon their action now; but at the time I was scandalised. With the fiery intolerance of youth I considered their interruptions an unpardonable sin, and the Salvation Army moved up towards the head of my list of criminals: a Gilbertian list which included the Kaiser, Lloyd George, and Mr Kensit, who in those days perseveringly endeavoured to persecute my father for his 'popish practices'.

My sensibilities were to be still further shocked. One Sunday morning my mother and I went to church as usual, and on reaching the Vicarage pew—third from the front on the right-hand side—found it already occupied by two strange young men. My mother asked them to move along, but they demurred and seemed about to refuse altogether when Mr Maule, a sidesman, hurried up and assumed a threatening demeanour in the background. At this the two men got up and took the seats nearest the centre aisle in the pew immediately in front of ours.

Mr Maule was a piano-tuner by profession, short, swarthy, and somewhat hirsute. There was nothing specially ferocious about his appearance; certainly nothing to reveal the fact that piano-tuning as an occupation produces an unusual strength of wrist in those who practice it perpetually. A concrete

F   81

application of this useful asset was to earn for him that morning my undying admiration.

During the service I regarded the strangers with unwavering suspicion. Their behaviour was anything but devout. They talked continually, not even in whispers, but in undertones, and seemed to be comparing notes about the service. They stared pointedly round the church, bobbed their heads and craned their necks to see what was happening in the chancel. Instead of kneeling properly, they remained seated, bending their bodies forward in the attitude of perfunctory humility known to us as the 'Protestant Crouch'. I had been brought up to 'kneel for worship, sit for instruction, and stand for praise'; and I found this piece of irreverence particularly offensive.

My suspicions were well-founded: they were Kensitites! At sermon-time my father had begun announcing his text when the man nearest the aisle—he was inclined to be fat and wore rimless spectacles—jumped to his feet and, turning very red, called out in a loud, strained voice: 'I wish to protest against this popish service held contrary to the laws of the Established Church!'

There was a shocked silence. The second young man looked very frightened, as though he wished he hadn't come and expected to be torn limb from limb. The first young man remained awkwardly standing with the air of having no idea what to do next. My father said in a cool, almost conversational tone from the pulpit: 'Mr Churchwarden, do your duty.' The young man began again loudly: 'I wish to protest——' The churchwarden had already started from his seat, but Mr Maule beat him by a short head. He picked up the first young man by his coat collar with one hand, and the second young man by his coat collar with the other, and carried them down the aisle, kicking feebly, like a pair of puppies who had misbehaved. I think he threw them down the steps outside the west door and told them exactly what

would happen to them if they dared to show their faces in
St Michael's Church again.

My heart had pounded uncomfortably during this exciting
incident, but my father continued his sermon as though
nothing had occurred: as he was to do so frequently some
thirty years later when the crash of German bombs was liable
to interrupt his remarks with as much discourtesy and no
more success.

To belong to the family of a clergyman is to establish a
certain modest but proprietary interest in the church itself.
The size of the congregations, the conduct of the services,
even the performance of the choir and organist acquire a
personal significance. A falling-off in numbers of the one or
quality of the other implied a criticism of my father: something I was unable to suffer yet powerless to remedy. At
least, it seemed so to me. But perhaps I was unduly sensitive.
After all, we lived much closer than the average laity to the
life of the Church; its seasons rolling past made as integral a
part of our days as the seasons of the year—more so, in
effect, for in a city slum the passing of winter into spring and
spring into high summer is scarcely less apparent than the
purple severities of Lent, the white and gold rejoicings of
Christmas or Easter, and the placid green flow of those
uneventful Sundays after Trinity.

And in the foreground of that solemn pageant, indeed, of
my existence, there moved the dominating figure of my father,
as familiar in the cassock and biretta of the daily service as in
the aged suits of 'clerical grey' he wore to go about the
unending business of that enormous parish.

5. The Sheet Anchor

Even allowing for the perfection that all parents attain in the estimation of their own children, I must have realised very early that my father was an unusual sort of person. Some people called him 'The Sporting Parson', because at Oxford he had played rugger and rowed for his College, while in his Poplar days he rode to hounds occasionally on a very large horse, Grey Ghost, kept specially for him in my grandfather's stables, played a good game of golf, and, until the end of his days, gave what spare time he could to his abiding passion of small-boat sailing. But the label was not apt, with its suggestion of the red-faced, the hearty and not over-intelligent 'muscular Christian'. If it described his geniality, his bubbling and irrepressible sense of humour, it did not define another facet of his vigorous personality: his deep knowledge of theology, his wide reading and constant study to keep himself in touch with every development in the world of church affairs.

And he was wise, with the inevitable wisdom of his great experience of human nature. Year by year he added to this

vast store of knowledge, as must any parish priest who lives
close to his people. You could see the wisdom behind his
eyes, whether they were smiling—as they most often were—
or grave and even stern, as they could sometimes be. Serious
or cheerful, they were always serene, as though from some
inner comfort that never left him.

He had a naturally friendly manner free from all trace of
condescension or false heartiness, and an unconventionality
which was essential in dealing with such parishioners as his.
He taught boxing and rugger to his Boys' Club, although
rugger frightened them to such an extent that a deputation
arrived at the Vicarage to ask if they might play soccer
instead, as rugger was so 'rough'! He went into the bars of
public-houses—with the reluctant consent of the landlords—
and held miniature mission services there with the surprised
customers as congregation: the sort of action courting ridi-
cule, contempt, and even blasphemy, that takes, in cold blood,
a handsome allowance of moral courage. On New Year's Eve
he would conduct a Watch Night Service in a crowded church,
although he always maintained the occasion to be strictly
secular and none of the Church's business. But its drawing-
power was indisputable and St Michael's would be packed to
the doors. If some had come because they could spend an
hour in warmth and dryness without cost, many more were
drawn to the church out of curiosity or sentiment. The public-
houses used to close about midnight and some of the congregation would be far from sober. Walking down the empty
church after one such service, my father found a little man,
dead-drunk, stretched out in a pew. Picking him up, he carried
him out of the west door where the people, slow to disperse,
were still chattering on the pavement.

'And who is the owner of this pretty thing?' he inquired,
holding out the unconscious form of the little drunk in his
arms. A large woman stepped out of the crowd to claim it,
addressing it in a shocked voice as 'George'. 'Oh, George,

what *'ave* you been up to?': a purely rhetorical query easily answerable by all present with the single exception of George himself.

This sort of spontaneity went straight to the hearts of those simple-minded people; and yet it might well have been said of my father that he was at his most effective in his church. Even after so many years I can think of few priests who can take a service better—or as well! Every word that he said could be heard with clarity; and he never resorted to the derided, but all too common lachrymose, parsonical intonation. He sang in tune; his tall, broad-shouldered figure showed off his vestments with impressive ease. He stripped the rites and ceremonies of any air of pomposity or theatricalism, performing them with the minimum of movement and the maximum of dignity. Not for him the actions designated by the detractors as 'bowings and scrapings'; he disliked the over-emphatic obeisance, the jerky genuflexion, the verging on the ludicrous indulged in by the unrestrained, as he abhorred anything unorthodox that smacked of the sensational or 'stunt', as it would be called today.

His sermons were models for any parish priest. He never preached for very long; and he never preached 'over people's heads'. He was no orator with a silver tongue, but he would get up in the pulpit and talk to his people, riveting their attention with a story, often making them laugh, always making them think; never assailing them with formless adjurations to 'be good', but invariably sending them away with some tangible addition to their spiritual knowledge, whether it were a piece of church history, doctrine, or the meaning of an ornament or ceremony. As illustrations he would employ any subject that appealed to him or served his purpose. There was a Christmas morning sermon in which my sister and I figured—anonymously, of course—to our abysmal shame. Some unusually enchanting presents—a toy railway, I suspect, in my own case—had fomented a tiny mutiny in the nursery. We did not want to go to church; we wanted to stay and play with our new possessions. The rebellion was crushed with ease; but not before my father got to hear of it, and quoted in his sermon some little girls he knew of who wished to enjoy all the material delights of Christmas while evading their obligations to the Almighty. We hung our heads in burning embarrassment; everyone, we felt sure, would know that he meant *us!*

Often he would use a scientific metaphor, especially an astronomical one, for the constellations, comets, stars and planets held for him a perennial fascination. When someone asked him the reason for this absorption in a hobby that, to say the least of it, was difficult to follow in the smoky atmosphere of Poplar, he replied: 'Well, I'm supposed to get my flock to heaven somehow, so I had better be familiar with the navigation marks!'

So often he must have felt his work to be fruitless and unrewarding, an eternal battering at unyielding walls of apathy and unbelief. Yet the church slowly filled, the choir boasted a waiting-list of applicants for membership, the roll of regular communicants lengthened steadily and confirmation classes increased in numbers. But his use and teaching of what would be regarded nowadays as the most usual practices of Anglo-Catholicism earned him many enemies, among them a local fanatic of the name of Owens, who, under the ægis of the Protestant Truth Society, held forth at great length and with considerable inexactitude upon my father's 'popish' activities.

There was nothing deliberately insulting in the fact that Owens chose to deliver himself of these diatribes in the open space under the Vicarage windows, because it happened to be the customary free forum of the whole neighbourhood. We were quite inured to listening to local politicians and the Salvation Army, agitators who informed their audiences that 'the Church lived on the earnings of the poor', and evangelists who dangled their hearers over the everlasting fires of hell. We put up even with pedlars of quack nostrums who needed more scope than Chrisp Street could afford. It was quite amusing to observe these demagogues stepping down from their little portable platforms and hurrying over to the nearest pub, while some sort of underling tried valiantly to hold the attention of the crowd for the length of time it took his principal to consume two pints.

But when it came to abuse, often of the most scurrilous kind, of my father, I boiled with rage. These meetings were usually held on fine summer evenings, long after I had been put to bed, and the ranting voice of Mr Owens came clearly through the open windows to annoy me. I would tiptoe across the landing and listen in the warm summer dusk behind a drawn blind to the flood of malicious nonsense.

If the audience proved apathetic to the enormity of my father's ritualistic crimes, then old Owens would do his best to sow the seeds of class-hatred by dilating upon his private means—modest enough, in all conscience—or his plutocratic hobbies.

'See how little he cares about us! While we're rotting here, pawning our last stick of furniture to buy a crust of bread for our starving kids, his lordship goes off, without a care in the world, to 'unt 'armless little foxes. He keeps a yacht, too, just for winning silver cups with, and the price of that yacht, let alone the cups, would keep a dozen Poplar families in coal and bread next winter!'

Mr Owens, incidentally, owned a comfortable little newsagent's shop, with tobacco and confectionery thrown in for good measure; and even in Poplar he was hardly likely to be starving. How I hated him! He bore a strong resemblance to an ageing and uncared-for goat, beard, long stringy neck, light cynical eyes and all. Only the steel-rimmed spectacles and an ability to talk balderdash—in a goat-like voice—differentiated him in my view from this unlovely animal.

Nanny, coming upstairs unexpectedly, would discover me sobbing with fury as I scuttled back across the landing at the sound of her footsteps. I would be tucked up, admonished, made to promise not to get out of bed again, and not to upset myself over Mr Owens, or Mr Kensit either, who sometimes came himself and repeated much the same string of accusations.

But I could only lie awake, taut with anger, and turn over in my mind the horrible punishments I would enjoy inflicting upon Mr Kensit and Mr Owens if only they could be delivered, bound and helpless, into my power. I would scalp them (after Fenimore Cooper); or stick red-hot needles into them; bring them slowly to the boil in a cauldron of water; and if only I could get them shipped out to Africa, I would have them pegged out to be devoured by soldier ants.

The accusations were specious enough, yet contained that grain of truth which made it impossible to ignore them altogether. My father *did* have a day's hunting now and again on Grey Ghost. He *did* keep a boat (scarcely to be glorified by the name of yacht) on the Thames and raced her on Saturday afternoons in summer. He won silver cups because he happened to be a skilful helmsman, but he was never a pot-hunter pure and simple. If my grandfather, a man of moderate wealth, chose to make him a small allowance to eke out the inadequate stipend of a poor London parish where there was neither endowment, nor rich tithes, and but a negligible Easter offering, a far higher proportion of that allowance than anyone could have guessed found its way into the parish. Time and time again he bought out of his own pocket furnishings or vestments for the church, and helped those in desperate straits for whom no existing charities or funds were available.

There was work and enough to keep ten parish priests fully occupied for seven days a week, but my father never had more than four curates at the peak of the parish fortunes, more usually only three; and at one time, soon after he came to Poplar, he had worked practically single-handed. The result of this complete neglect of self was the foregone conclusion only to be expected from a temperament that had to work in top gear or not at all: a severe nervous breakdown with all the distressing concomitants of amnesia, insomnia, and acute neuritis.

We children realised little of what was happening at the time, the only symptom of deterioration in his health to affect us being a certain deterioration in his temper. But my mother must have undergone agonies of apprehension and pity when she was obliged to sit under the pulpit, outwardly calm, and listen to him groping vainly for the words that would not come. On one occasion, and in the presence of the Bishop, there was a complete collapse. Having given out his text and spoken a few halting phrases, he was compelled to say: 'I am sorry, but I cannot remember any more,' and leave the pulpit.

My mother was always at her best in times of crisis; her serene nature and gentle courage must have been the ideal antidote for the strain of overwork and worry. The Bishop of London was entirely sympathetic, for Arthur Foley Winnington-Ingram knew and cherished his clergy—and their families—as perhaps few diocesans have done before or since. Six months of complete idleness was necessary before my father was able to work again; and as a kind of insurance against any future repetition of such a calamity, he was strictly enjoined by the doctors on his return to take one entire day away from the parish every week: no more, in fact, than the equivalent of the layman's Sunday.

And it was out of this modest concession to the demands of health that the apostles of protestantism tried to make their grubby capital. A cardinal weakness in their case was their failure to admit that my father came to Poplar of his own deliberate choice. Pleading his young family, he could have remained with a clear conscience to work in a more salubrious spot. But the bitter bigotry of religious animosity could give no quarter. The persecutions went on ceaselessly; my father was even, at one time, the defendant in a prosecution for alleged 'illegal papist usages: to wit, that he did wear an alb; to wit, that he did wear one girdle', and all the rest of the hocus-pocus dressed up in the solemn jargon of the law. He was, of course, acquitted. His defence was impregnable: a simple matter of a few lines of print in an obscure corner of the Book of Common Prayer. He had performed no ceremony nor worn any vestment not fully sanctioned by the Ornaments Rubric as according to the proper usage of the Church of England. The plaintiffs had omitted to take into their calculations the First Prayer Book of King Edward the Sixth (quite possibly they had never heard of it); and the case was among the last attempts of the Protestant Truth Society to bring such actions into prominence in a court of law.

Nowadays it seems positively ludicrous that anyone in their right minds should have thought it worth while to go to law about such trivialities as the colour of a cassock, the depth of a genuflexion, and the number of candlesticks upon an altar. But in those calm Edwardian days, when there were no major political or scientific problems to distract the mind, nothing more alarming in the headlines of newspapers than the eternal quarrels of the Balkan States and the laughable impertinence of the Germans in daring to challenge our supremacy at sea, people bickered with acrimony and violence over such minor issues of party politics and religious observance as would be lost today in the floods of ideological warfare.

The senseless annoyance of the prosecution added to the strain from which my father was already suffering must have made a heavy contribution to the final collapse. Yet he recovered from it all with a typical resilience of spirit and body. From his six months of rest—spent principally in boats —he came back to Poplar, restored in health and with a renewed zest for work: back to the ugly but beloved church—

which he and my mother longed unavailingly to beautify—to the grimy Vicarage, to the squalid streets, the smoke and the smells; and above all, to the people who had begun by now to trust him and to love him, to feel confidence in his power to shoulder their burdens.

Sometimes the Vicarage door-bell would peal in the middle of the night, for a parson, like a doctor, can be called at any hour. Often it would be the expected summons to the bedside of the dying; but now and again, at long, irregular intervals, my father would find shivering on the doorstep the ragged figure of a little, shrivelled old man. In a hoarse whisper he would explain his errand.

'I've got it coming on again, guv'nor. Can you help me?'

'It' was the compulsion to take his own life, and the suppliant a retired sailor whom my father had prevented from jumping into 'the Cut' one cold, dark, winter's day. The little old man was not entirely without money, but like many people who have led a rootless existence, he was singularly friendless, and there were times when the impulse to commit suicide very nearly overcame the remnants of his common sense. There was but one thing to do.

'Guv'nor, you're my sheet anchor,' he would say. 'I know it's wicked, but it's powerful strong when it comes over me. I tells myself, if I can but get to see the guv'nor, I shall put it astern of me.'

And so, whenever he heard the whispered plea for help across the threshold of our house, my father would say: 'Come in, come in! We'll sit by the fire and have a chat.'

Or in summer-time he would walk with him patiently up and down the streets, until dawn if need be, until such time as the old sailorman would declare that the struggle was over; the secret enemy had passed and he had nothing to be afraid of any more; and go off again to his solitary existence like a child who, scared by bad dreams, needs company for a while before he can face the darkness.

Such was my father's work: to preach the faith he professed, and to help and comfort the sick, the weary, and the overburdened; and for this he had been ordained, rather than to be pricked by the petty animosities of the bigots.

His people called him 'Father' with ease; to them the appellation seemed entirely natural and appropriate. To my sister and I, his physical children, he presented not only all those facets of his character—the benignity, the rock-like reliability, the forbearance and compassion—but also the exhilarating manifestations of an eternally youthful spirit. Not only in the docks had you to be prepared for something exciting to happen when in his company; not only was it with him that we were initiated into such joys as the theatre, and the new-fangled moving-pictures. He was the instigator of our amusements and the originator of all sorts of adventures, escapades, indeed of all the more outstanding experiences of our infant lives.

Even that hour before bed-time in the study was transformed by his ingenuity. Until I was quite of a reasonable age—possibly eight or even nine—he continued to mystify and enchant me by means of a trick—the most transparent trick into the bargain—known as the trick of the Disappearing Penny, for which I begged over and over again. With the usual mumbo-jumbo of magic passes and 'Hey Prestos!' he would 'palm' the penny. It had vanished beyond doubt; I could find it nowhere. I would be bidden to look for it in the bath, and I would stump upstairs, shrieking with joy and excitement, with anticipation that the coin would be there, with dread that the magic might have failed and it would not. It was *there!* It was always there, lying innocently in the bottom of the bath. I could hardly get downstairs quick enough, to press it into my father's hand with triumph. I never had the gumption to grasp that it had been placed in the bath beforehand, nor the wit to see that it did not necessarily tally with the original penny. My sense of deflation, when at last I learned the simple explanation, was profound.

Then there was the curious and extraordinary episode of 'the Nightbirds'. One winter's evening fire broke out in a factory sufficiently close to the Vicarage for us to see the flames leaping upwards and to hear the roar and crackle as they devoured the place with greedy appetite. Everyone in Poplar always stopped whatever they were doing and rushed to see the fire-engines go by as soon as they heard the clattering of hooves and the clanging of bells. The horses galloped at full tilt, foam on their muzzles; the urgent ringing of the bell seemed to fill the narrow streets, echoing back from the house-fronts; the brass helmets of the firemen shone with a martial glint; and from a cylindrical object at the back of the engine came the sinister red glow of burning coals. The purpose of this contrivance, I imagined, was to spur on the wretched horses to still further effort; not until much later did I discover that it was a kind of boiler in which steam was raised to provide pressure for the hoses!

Fires were common among the jerry-built houses, but this was the largest we had ever known. It soared ever higher into the night sky; huge flaming fragments hurtled over the roofs, borne on a strong wind; and since it was blowing in our direction, there was even talk of hanging wet blankets over the Vicarage windows on that side of the house. No one seemed to have noticed that my bed-time was drawing near, so that when my father announced that he was going out to have a look at the fire, I was emboldened to grasp his coat-tails and clamour to go with him. To my immense surprise, he was willing to take me. My mother protested vainly; Nanny, clearly disapproving, grumbled as she bundled me into boots, bonnet, coat and muffler. Routine had gone by the board, adventure was in the air, and we set off as fast as my short legs would go in their endeavour to keep up with my father's lengthy stride.

The patter of many running feet in the darkness pointed the way as clearly as the blaze itself, for a fire provided the populace with a splendid free spectacle. As we drew near it was obvious that this was no ordinary fire; the crowd was large and the helmets of many policemen were silhouetted against the glare. My father spoke to someone in a peaked cap and I caught the word 'looting' spoken low over my head. Then my father lifted me to his shoulder, where I was high above the crowd and free of that suffocating sensation of being crushed that children experience in a press of people.

At first I had eyes only for the fire and the concentration of engines brought to fight it. Then something made me look at the faces of those watching all around us. From that height and in that glow as bright as daylight I could see them clearly, and while some were ordinary enough, there were others that struck me with a kind of creeping terror. They were barely human. They had one thing in common—an intense pallor, a thick, uniform whiteness that reminded me of my mother's indoor bulbs when she first brought them out of the cellar. I saw a face all nose, a great beak of a nose above a thread-like mouth and a chin scarcely perceptible; its eyes were hooded by deep fleshy folds. Another was dominated by a snout, pierced by distended nostrils and so flattened that, with its heavy hanging jowls, it resembled nothing so much as the pig's head on a butcher's counter. The forehead was so low and narrowed to such a point that the hair came almost to the eyebrows above tiny eyes set in rings of fat. Another was all long, lean, bony muzzle with hollow cheeks and a small pointed chin. A dog? A fox? No, a wolf, such as I saw in the Zoo pacing tirelessly up and down its cage. As though feeling my gaze upon him, the Wolf Man turned his head and stared at me as though I were as strange to him as he to me. The eyes were fierce, sharp, cruel and wary; there was also something queer about them which I could not then assess. Now that recollection can interpret my sensations, I fancy I got the extraordinary idea that there was nothing behind those eyes. Meeting the average individual's glance, even when he is putting up his defences, you are aware of the actual person, the living being who looks out at you; but in the case of those odd, sub-human people on the night of the fire, the house was without a tenant, the windows empty and blank.

I did not feel much physical fear, a virtual impossibility in my father's company; but I did feel for the first time in my life the concrete presence of evil. Not until the fire was obviously under control did we turn towards home, and my father did not set me down on the pavement until we were well clear of the crowd. He hadn't put me up on his shoulder, he said, entirely for my convenience, but because my feet hanging down helped to protect his money from pickpockets; I should have noticed at once if anyone had tried to take his pocket-book. Scurrying along beside him, hanging on to his hand like grim death—just in case the Wolf Man might be close behind us—I asked breathlessly if there had been pick-pockets at the fire.

'Of course! Fires always bring them out—they can pick people's pockets at their leisure because the owners are busy looking at the fire,' he said. 'Didn't you notice those people with funny faces? They were the night-birds—never see the light of day, never come out until night-time, except for something like a big fire. That's why they're so pale, like something that lives under a stone. They're bad people, all right!'

He was very sensible; he never tried to minimise things, or gloss over the worst side of life in Poplar. Presently he chuckled.

'It's long past your bedtime! I'm going to catch it from your mother!'

We 'caught it', but only very lightly: a gentle remonstrance from my mother, a mild display of displeasure by Nanny, who nevertheless was extremely interested to hear about the fire as she bathed me, did my hair up in 'curl-rags', and popped me into bed in double-quick time.

Tucked up and comfortable, with my briar-pipe (needless to say, unsmoked, but the most masculine symbol I could procure as opposed to dolls or teddy-bears) pushed carefully under the pillow, I wondered a little fearfully if my dreams would be haunted by that repulsive and sinister trio, the Pig Man, the Hawk Man and the Wolf Man: the Night-birds! But it seemed that they had no place in the serenity of the Vicarage, where the day, placid yet busy, was drawing to its normal end. In the nursery next-door Nanny was singing hymns softly to herself in her good Welsh voice while she did the day's mending. Agreeable smells of cooking rose up the well of the stairs; there was the chink of plates, and then the sound of Elizabeth beating cautiously on the gong: dinner was being served and eaten.

Here, in this minute citadel of the conventions, the cushioned Edwardian life went on because, quite naturally, it had never occurred to my mother that a house could be run in any other fashion. Here the settled, immutable routine of meals, of 'doing the orders', of rooms 'turned out' on regular days, of morning prints and starched white caps and aprons, of the tiny hierarchy, carefully observed, of nursery and kitchen, pursued its way calmly but tenaciously: a lighted bastion of the established and the secure set prosaically against the darkness in which the Night-birds, servants of Satan himself, prowled seeking whom they might devour!

I did not fear them. Over the night-nursery mantelpiece hung a crucifix; St Michael's was at my elbow; at any moment my father would come to say good night. He had promised that he would come—'as soon as you're asleep!'

It was years before I saw the catch.

6. Born in the Cloth

BETWEEN the church and the Vicarage, entered with ease from either, lay a sort of No Man's Land of a room, used, before my father built the Parish Hall, for various parochial meetings and known as the Committee Room. About it there hung perpetually the smell of unwashed bodies and clothes that have been worn too long, with which we were so familiar: the smell of poverty and the smell of Poplar—fifty years ago.

Once the Hall in Ullin Street had been constructed, all parish functions were held therein; no longer needed, the Tumty Room (as it was pronounced by myself) became available as an extra sitting-room for the incumbent and his family.

On Sundays after Evensong all the curates came to supper in the Tumty Room. The strong scent of their tobacco smoke and the rumble of their deep bass laughter rose even to the distant night-nursery. Relaxed after a hard Sunday, they seemed to laugh a great deal; the supper-parties, I thought, must be very jolly, although I wondered what they found to laugh about. To the Tumty Room, on Christmas Eve, I would descend, feeling faintly sick with excitement, to behold the wonderful spectacle of the Tree hung with presents; and it was in the Tumty Room, as I grew older, that I set about the laborious business of acquiring a wider education.

Nanny had taught me to read and write at the age of four. In the mornings, before Nanny was ready to go out, I had applied myself without enthusiasm but with ultimate success, to the correct execution of pot-hooks and hangers, the penning of such desirable copy-book maxims as 'A stitch in time saves nine', or 'The devil finds work for idle hands to do'. At night, in that delicious, sleepy quarter of an hour before going to the bath, sitting on Nanny's knee beside the nursery fire, I would spell out the Beatrix Potter books, Struwelpeter—'the good dog Tray grew very red'—and the Christmas Annuals. She also taught me to add, subtract, and multiply; and more than that in the sphere of mathematics no one has ever been able to accomplish. Then I was supposed to learn by heart small portions of that remarkable work of edification, *A Child's Guide to Knowledge*, compiled 'By a Lady', which, in the form of prim little questions and rather priggish replies conveys all sorts of odd and astonishingly variegated facts about the world as seen by mid-Victorian eyes.

But I was achieving no real progress in my learning, and at length my mother decided that I should have proper morning lessons. Well-qualified governesses, I suppose, could not be persuaded easily to brave the ferocious dangers of the East End streets, and she began to teach me herself.

My mother came of a family of scholars, theologians and archæologists, dedicated to the professions and a love of learning for learning's sake. As a girl she studied Greek by correspondence course 'for fun', and read the *Anglo-Saxon Chronicle* in its original script for pleasure. Born into a later generation she would have achieved automatically a brilliant degree and academic distinction. But her parents declined to consider seriously the suggestion that she should go to one

of the women's colleges, suspect as breeding-grounds of
feminism and even of suffragettes; and her talent for impart-
ing knowledge was thus compressed into the single receptacle
of one small child's mind.

Our curriculum, so far as I can remember, was neither
extensive nor regular. Arithmetic had no interest for my
mother; besides, women scarcely needed more mathematical
ability than was necessary to compute the household accounts.
Botany was an unprofitable subject to pursue in that wilder-
ness of bricks and mortar where you would have been hard
put to it to provide a genuine specimen outside the seedsmen's
boxes in the Chrisp Street Market. We studied geography,
however—perfunctorily on my part, I confess, but then I have
never been able to learn anything about a country except by
travelling to it. I would look at the large red portions on
Mercator's Projection and think how admirable it would be
to have the whole world coloured red. The rule of Britain
seemed to me entirely beneficent and I could not understand
the strange reluctance of other countries to come under its
sheltering umbrella, their obstinate determination to remain
green, brown, or yellow upon the map, and to retain their
own habits and customs, so immensely inferior to ours.
'Little Englanders', when I learned about them, shocked me
indescribably; I could not imagine why King Edward the
Seventh did not have them all hanged as traitors.

Much of our time was taken up by history—and history
taught, as I can realise now, in the most personal and
romantic fashion. Here my mother's passion for the past
could indulge itself up to the hilt. Moreover, we went very
far back into the past, for in her opinion, history should start,
not with William the Conqueror and the Romans, but at the
very beginning of things. Stone, Iron, and Bronze Age men
peopled my lessons; Jurassic, Eocene, and Pleistocene periods
rolled over my head in all the splendour of their magnificent
syllables, although, beyond privately identifying the last-

named with a well-known make of modelling clay, I doubt if I grasped their real significance. In this sort of perspective, Boadicea became a comparatively modern personage, the Roman occupation of Britain a recent happening. Listening to my mother's voice, low and gentle, as she described with the fervour of an enthusiast those monuments to the power of Rome still to be seen in Britain, such as Hadrian's Wall, Bath, York and Colchester, I wished earnestly that a real, live Roman centurion would materialise before me—as he had done to Una in *Puck of Pook's Hill*—although I suspected uneasily that St Leonard's Road was deplorably unlikely ground for such an apparition.

As for the Plantagenets and Tudors, I became familiar with them through the Plays of Shakespeare, which my mother would read to me out of thick, heavy, dark-green volumes. These were copiously annotated, illustrated by engravings which even then appeared old-fashioned to my eyes, and printed in curiously archaic type on yellowing paper which possessed a richly fusty smell—a highly 'bookish' smell, summoning to my mind the vision of an enormous library inhabited by learned dons who read the plays very slowly while engaged in smoking cigars—dropping the ash on their waistcoats—and drinking tall, thin bottles of light, Rhine wine. Some of the plays seemed long and tedious, and I could not always understand what they were about; but the sweep and flow of the language could not be disguised, surging through one's head like a tide.

All at once the lesson-hour would be over, and Nanny would be standing in the Tumty Room doorway saying prosaically: 'Come along. It's time for your walk.'

What had I learnt? Little, probably, in actual fact; an immense amount by inference, in that I grew up on nodding terms with a vast range of names and places: the names of classical literature, of writers, painters, sculptors, saints and emperors; the sites of ancient capitals and the scenes of great events, which in the past so often seemed to consist of battles, sieges, martyrdoms and executions. In so many words, I acquired the boon of general knowledge, an asset—if from no other than the social standpoint—noticeably lacking nowadays.

My parents' general knowledge must have been prodigious. Apart from the normal education of their kind, they read insatiably with a catholicity of interests and never allowed their brains to rust with inactivity. My father read the Bible in the original Greek and Hebrew until the very last years of his life; he read habitually theology, history, philosophy and science with an emphasis on astronomy; for relaxation he turned to books about ships and yachting, especially the art and science of boat-building and design.

In addition to her two main subjects, history and archæology, my mother favoured biography and travel. But they both read novels, if the spirit moved them, by such authors as E. F. Benson and Somerset Maugham; even the contemporary equivalent of 'thrillers' by Conan Doyle and Seton Merriman; their intellectual life was by no means always spent at the highest levels. As for their children, we were encouraged to read anything and everything; nothing was ever taken away from us with the remark: 'That's much too grown-up for you; you won't understand that.'

My father, energetic and smiling, strides purposefully across the foreground of the Poplar scene; but, characteristically, it is in the background, or at best the middle distance, that one must look for the figure of my mother, drawn in dry-point and tinted with pastels. Not that she is in the least a vague or ineffectual sort of person; but it is in the background, I fancy, that she has always preferred to remain: gentle where he was vigorous, static where he was mobile, passive where he was positive, smiling, too—but a little sadly, for she has inherited the faint but agreeable strain of melancholy of a double line of Celtic forbears.

Nothing is further from her nature than hurry, bustle,

impetuosity; hers is not the temperament to initiate new ventures, but rather to listen, advise, and encourage the enterprise of others. It is clearly apparent to me now that placidity and receptiveness have always been her two predominating characteristics; but to a child the most noticeable thing about her was a sort of constancy, a quality of dependableness which naturally increased later when we were obliged to part with Nanny. It seems that she was always *there* when you wanted her, at home, working in the garden or stitching at the beautiful embroidery that she only abandoned in her mid-eighties when her sight began to fail.

Of what enormous value to the young is this constant factor of maternal attentiveness! A whole period of her life can be described, on her own admission, as taken up with listening for voices—the voices of her family calling 'Mother' —and later still 'Grannie'—'where are you?' But in Poplar she was much occupied with the affairs of that vast, importunate parish, with the work for which, as a clergyman's daughter, she had been well prepared.

All her life had been spent in the country until, her hopes of a university career having vanished, she came to London, joining a voluntary organisation known, by reason of their grey cloaks and bonnets, as Grey Ladies. The desire to help those in greatest need was still very strong even at the end of a century which had produced in its earliest decades the Industrial Revolution and its wretched but logical consequence, the city slum. These unselfish women lived among the poorest and most over-crowded districts, devoting their lives to visiting the sick and destitute. Inevitably, they saw something of the parish clergy; and thus my parents met. With her singularly classic profile and serious grey eyes, my mother, tall and slender, must have made a striking figure in that unbecoming cloak and bonnet against a background of the less reputable streets of Peckham. The handsome and energetic curate had most of the young ladies of the parish running after him, but my mother was not among them. She had never contemplated marriage; the womenfolk of her family inclined traditionally to spinsterdom; and no one was more surprised than she when the good-looking young curate proposed to *her*, for she was expecting daily to hear the announcement of his engagement to someone else!

There is something to be said for recruiting a wife from the ranks of parsons' daughters. She has been born in the cloth, so to speak, and brought up in the peculiar atmosphere —not necessarily rarefied, either, as lay-folk might imagine— of the vicarage or rectory, and is therefore better qualified to inhabit for the rest of her life those rambling and usually down-at-heel abodes in which the pursuit of heaven and the proffering of spiritual advice are curiously intermingled with requests for discarded clothing and the incumbent's signature. She comprehends from the beginning the semi-public existence of the parish priest who is always at the service, not only of his own conscience but of the sick and the troubled among his flock; and she has learnt to perfection her proper place in the parochial pattern.

She should be indefinite in personality, not too opinionated, aggressive, or distinctive. Her protective colouring should be sub-fusc, therefore, she should be neatly, but never too smartly, dressed; she should wear suitable clothes suggesting poverty and unworldliness, but not so shabby as to prove an embarrassment to those she is with. The comfortably-off parishioner is easily affronted by the spectacle of the vicar's wife in clothes as good, or better than, her own, especially when she is supposed to contribute to the vicar's Easter offering! Naturally, the wife should be willing to perform the less agreeable tasks about the church and parish that time and tradition have long ago allocated as her portion: mending the hassocks or the choir-boys' cassocks; polishing those awkward bits of brass; running the Mothers' Meeting and taking on the unattractive kind of stall at the annual Sale of Work. She should be prepared to do the altar decorations in the middle of the winter, when flowers are terribly expensive and very scarce; but she mustn't be greedy and expect to do them in the summer as well, when everybody's gardens are blooming and it's quite enjoyable to fill the church with great *splashes* of colour—hydrangeas and peonies, delphiniums and phlox.

She is, of course, necessary to the smooth running of the parsonage: her existence prevents the gossip provoked by almost any type of housekeeper, however old or hideous, and safeguards the laity from a tiresome sense of obligation: 'Oh, dear, I wonder how that poor man is getting on in that barn of a rectory. He looks awfully thin; do you think we ought to ask him in to supper?'

She should, in fact, be entirely functional, like a good, strong chair to be sat upon, or a plain, serviceable carpet that will stand a great deal of wear; and she must not be allowed to think too well of herself.

'The parson has to have a wife, no doubt, and we'd better ask her to tea, but don't let's have her to dinner, there's no need for that!'

My mother never forgot, and would repeat with some amusement, the admonitions of a bishop's wife to a gathering of young clergy wives belonging to her husband's diocese. They must not expect, she told them with a fine complacent patronage, to be asked to *dine* at the Squire's house; it would be sufficient, and very gracious, if he and his wife acknowledged their existence by inviting them to the Hall for parochial functions such as Garden Fêtes, etc. In strict parenthesis, it might be said that my mother's family themselves occupied the position of squire of the neighbourhood in a certain district of Oxfordshire. Mercifully, this attitude of appalling condescension to the clergy by lay-folk and—though more rarely—by the higher ecclesiastics, has been modified by time, the transformation of the social structure, and to some extent, by apathy.

Inevitably a revolt has taken place against the conception of the parson's wife as 'unpaid curate'; since nowadays she has to do much of her own housework—if not all—clearly she cannot be expected to undertake a great deal in the parish. But those who have swung the pendulum too far the other way by dissociating themselves completely from their husbands' professional activities, as though they were the wives of stockbrokers or actuaries, bring just condemnation on their heads.

Fortunately for my mother, that odious brand of nineteenth-century snobbery could never grow in Poplar; the conditions under which it could take root and flourish were simply non-existent. Things were usually so bad there that people accepted help with gratitude—but not with cringing subservience and while still preserving their independence—without bothering their heads over where it came from. When the waters of destitution are about to close over your head, you don't inquire the social status of the persons who throw you a rope in the shape of food-tickets made out on the few good shops in the district. When the breadwinner has been out on strike for weeks, the children are famished and you are expecting another baby, you don't particularly care whether the vicar's wife hands you a plate of meat-stew with the proper amount of humility, or whether the stew is made from 'scraps' at twopence a pound from the Chrisp Street stalls—which is more than you could afford, in any case.

Feeding these expectant mothers in the Parish Hall during the dismal strikes and lock-outs of that disturbed industrial decade was an activity that particularly concerned my mother; her greatest difficulty was to prevent the women smuggling out the stew in some receptacle for their hungry husbands to eat at home!

Peckham followed by Poplar should have toughened her susceptibilities and destroyed the last of her illusions about human nature. On the contrary, she remained compassionate, selfless, and curiously innocent. Often the target of abuse by the very people she was trying to help, she used to admit that she simply did not understand the words that were shouted at her; Greek would have been infinitely more intelligible! Brought up in the quiet, pleasant, even humdrum life of Victorian country rectories, the sights and sounds of London slums must inevitably have shocked her. You would have expected her to say to herself: 'What on earth am I, offspring of a peaceful and pious home, doing in this verminous room in a stinking back-alley in one of the worst slums in East London?' But I doubt if she ever did. Her good sense, and her extreme innocence must have carried her through all sorts of situations that someone less well-balanced or more sophisticated would have found intolerable.

She had to perform the most extraordinary tasks that must have been quite foreign to her nature and worlds remote from her upbringing: as when, at the end of a prolonged strike and armed with a prodigious bunch of pawn-tickets, she 'redeemed' from the pawn-shops of Poplar the wedding-rings of some of the unfortunate dockers' wives.

Many of her activities were the normal routine of any vicar's wife. The membership of her Mothers' Meeting ran into several hundred, a proportion of whom, she suspected, attended the gatherings in the Parish Hall for the sake of an afternoon's 'sit down' in a warm room, and the cup of tea with a biscuit for which my mother paid out of her own pocket: to have charged the customary pence might have wrecked the precarious family budget. Then there was the question of the annual outing, a summer day's expedition to some spot in the country which had to be within easy reach of London, for they went in horse-drawn brakes.

The sight of these vehicles 'picking up' outside the Vicarage was no novelty to me, for so many excursions started from that convenient place. Something faintly reminiscent of the rural, perhaps of the hay-wain from which they had descended, seemed to linger about these splendid conveyances, far less comfortable but infinitely more imposing than the stream-lined char-à-bancs, the chromium-plated caterpillar that has replaced them. They were very high off the ground; their sides were often brightly painted, the spokes of the large wheels picked out handsomely in red or yellow. In the grander sort, there was an awning that could be pulled over all; and they were drawn usually by two chestnut horses, to which the adjectives 'spanking' or 'high-spirited' could scarcely be applied with perfect truth.

The women would climb the steep little ladder at the back with much tittering and bunching of ground-length Edwardian skirts. In the more uproarious parties—*never*, of course, St Michael's Mothers' Meeting—a visit would already have been paid to the pub for a refresher or a bracer before the trip began, and there would be some competition to sit next to the driver who, like most London bus-drivers, would be fat, florid, and a tremendous wit: in any case, a fine figure of a man as he surveyed the world from the authoritative posi-tion of his lofty seat. Off they would go to the sound of shrieks, laughter, cheers, catcalls from those left behind, the cracking of the driver's whip and the thunder of the horses' hooves as they got the whole contraption under way. The return home at night was a spectacle worth watching for: feathered hats would be askew, boas trailing carelessly over the sides, faces flushed, the men's jackets off, perhaps a fight going on in the rear seats. And they sang—heavens, how they sang! With enough force, fury, fervour and sentiment to crack their vocal cords and split their throats. No wonder they were so thirsty, I thought, and had to take so many bottles of beer and stout with them, from which they drank adroitly as they rolled along.

The St Michael's women, accompanied by my mother, naturally never engaged in such indecorous displays. They had to be content with a good tea and a walk round the unaccustomed country lanes before returning in time to put 'the kids' to bed: very small beer compared to the mammoth Sunday school outing when a thousand children shepherded by the clergy, their teachers and some of the parents travelled to the sea by special train. My mother would be roped in for this strenuous event as well, since many grown-ups were needed to keep in order this huge flock of boys and girls, all wild with excitement at the prospect of a day by the sea. Pulling the alarm-cord of the train was their greatest joy, next to hanging out of the windows, a privilege for which they fought incessantly. The danger lay in the door-fastenings of the period, large brass handles which one lifted up to open. An inadvertent kick or carelessly raised knee would be quite enough to shift them, and the adults went in perpetual dread of serious accidents.

But only once in all those years was there a tragedy: on the journey to Southend—the favourite destination—a small boy fell from the train. It was stopped at once, and my father ran back along the line to pick up the body; my mother, seeing the fair-haired head lolling limply from his arms, knew that the child was dead.

The excursion went on, but my father came back alone to tell the boy's parents; he also dashed into the Vicarage to change his clothes, which were soaked in blood. I could not understand why he had returned so unexpectedly, nor why I was not allowed to 'bother' him. With the fatal inquisitiveness of a child, I looked into the bathroom and saw his shirt floating in a bathful of pale scarlet water. This sent me bawling back to Nanny, convinced that my beloved father had been badly hurt; and since I did not learn the truth until the evening, I was well punished, as Nanny severely informed me, for 'poking my nose into things that didn't concern me!'

At Christmas the Sunday School was also bidden to a lavish Annual Christmas Tea in the Parish Hall, at which every child crammed itself to bursting point with food and was the recipient of a toy. This meant a great deal of work for my mother, who would begin about November to write to all her relatives and personal friends with families of their own asking for their discarded toys. The response would be so great that a steady stream of toys would arrive at the Vicarage, to be stored, first in the Tumty Room, and later in the Parish Hall. I used to regard the mounting piles of these gifts with a disgruntled and a jealous eye, despite the old ottoman in the nursery that was literally stuffed with toys. Children have no natural instinct for generosity; acquisitiveness and avarice are their automatic reactions where property is concerned. They are born Forsytes! Although I was intensely sorry for the ragged, hungry children of Poplar, I do not remember that it ever occurred to me to part with any of my playthings for their benefit, unless prompted to do so, somewhat grudgingly, by some pretty forceful hints from Nanny!

One, at least, of my mother's activities on behalf of children was to prove of lasting value. Child mortality was then extremely high, thanks to the ignorance of the mothers of the most elementary hygienic principles and the complete lack of what would now be regarded as essential amenities in the brick hovels which were their homes. Infinitely disturbed by this grievous waste of life, educated people were forming Health Visiting Associations in slum areas all over London. The need was felt to be so desperate that these organisations, staffed entirely by voluntary workers drawn from the ranks of most Christian creeds, were instantly successful. My mother served on a large committee in the Poplar district, carrying out her share of visiting in the poorest homes, where sound advice could at least be proffered, even if it was not always well received or followed. The work was gruelling and often disagreeable, a kind of slogging match between ignorance, indifference or despair on the one hand, and goodwill reinforced by tact, patience and knowledge on the other. The volunteers tramped in all weathers about the filthy courts and alleys, climbed innumerable rickety flights of bug-ridden stairs; they had their reward at the end of the first twelve months of these endeavours, when the death-rate among children revealed a slight but unmistakable fall—to be maintained and steadily increased in years to come.

When the government of the day eventually awoke to the true state of affairs and created an official Health Department, its construction and methods were largely based on the records and experience of the Health Visiting Associations.

As in every poor parish, much of my mother's time was taken up with the necessity for raising money: money to buy materials for the Vicarage working-party, so that more money could be made at the annual Church Bazaar; money to buy flowers with which to decorate the church, for the faithful of St Michael's could not afford such a luxury. Many of her friends living in the country would send her flowers, particularly at the great festivals; but for the altar vases, week by week, she herself was invariably responsible.

Her life was very full. She had her household to manage and her children to consider; she gave some attention even to her patch of deplorable garden, in which nothing would grow save purple flag-iris, tiger-lilies, and appropriately enough, a flourishing crop of London Pride. It was, perhaps, a curious existence for someone of her tastes and education, whose preferences lay in the direction of heraldry, fine embroidery, the Renaissance painters and Greek classical literature. Provided by her Celtic inheritance with plenty of imagination, she would nevertheless have set about those odd kinds of activity with matter-of-factness and a minimum of fuss. Whatever was sensible, expedient, most needing to be done, that she would do. And yet she has never been severely practical in the usual meaning of the phrase: not naturally skilled and handy, unlike my father, who was the most finished carpenter and with sufficient practice could have turned out real cabinet-makers' jobs.

Not that she admits for one moment to any lack of such a quality. No sooner were they grown-up than she and her sisters, with that *fin de siècle* reverence for the handicrafts that distinguished a period in which machinery had established its ascendancy so indisputably, attended classes in etching, wood-carving, and beaten metal-work. The earnestness, the gentle determination of the proceeding, simply for the purpose of acquiring a physical skill, a 'craft', is nearly incomprehensible to a later generation compelled, willy-nilly, by force of circumstance, to use their hands. Neither had she much leisure, in Poplar, at any rate, to fill with such pursuits, although on our summer holidays she would achieve some delightful and talented water-colour sketches.

The life was as far divorced as possible from the fashionable round of Lancaster Gate: the leaving of cards, the tea-parties, the musical soirées, Monday 'Pops' at Queen's Hall, the Ring at Covent Garden. Had she many regrets? Impossible to say; but to anyone with such a high sense of duty and total disregard of self, I imagine that they were few: perhaps no more than a passing nostalgia for the pretty clothes that were so unsuitable in Poplar. She had never been what is known as 'smart', nor given much thought to dress beyond a normal woman's desire to wear what is charming and what becomes her. Obviously, no one with the slightest regard for decency could wear anything in Poplar save the plainest garments; and these, as I have recorded, were often slightly shabby; they have left little impression on my mind save of sombre colours and severe cut.

And yet there is one dress that I remember because it stands out amongst the rest, and one recollection of my mother wearing it that I retain more vividly than most, probably because I received its impress at the moment between waking and sleeping when the visual memory seems to be especially sensitive.

I had been put to bed, and she and my father had come to

say good night to me before going out to dinner in their old parish 'up West': doubtless I would refuse to go to sleep until I had seen them 'all dressed up'. They stood at my bed-side, looking very tall to my drowsy gaze, my father in the glossy black expanse of his clerical evening waistcoat, my mother in a trailing dinner-gown of fine white lace and smell-ing of lavender water: an elegant couple, and truly Edwardian, returning for a few hours to the world of parties and At Homes upon which they had so resolutely turned their backs.

7. A Piece of Tarred Twine

I CAME into the world with a considerable handicap, common to millions of girl-babies before and since: I was to have been a boy, and I was to have been dedicated to the sea.

A strong salt-water strain ran through the veins of my father's family, although they had little or no professional connection with the sea. A passion for all things maritime informed them, almost without exception; yet the only near relative to follow the sea as a career was that Great-uncle Reginald who had served in sail, and according to tradition, had distinguished himself by becoming mate in the famous *Sobraon*.

I fancy that my father's love of the sea was only just outweighed by his sense of vocation for the Church. Be that as it may, the Church won; but the sea never relinquished its hold on him throughout his entire life, and he died within sight and sound of it and, like many a good sailorman before him, at the exact hour when the ebb-tide had started to run out.

But the sea-career which he had never chosen for himself

was to be followed by a son; the plans were laid in earnest during the summer that my parents awaited their second child: a long, hot summer in which, as it happened, they grew heartily tired of waiting for me to put in an appearance, and when I eventually did so, I was the wrong sex into the bargain. But my father, always an optimist, took heart and decided with his usual single-minded enthusiasm to make the best of a bad job. He determined that, even if I were debarred from professional seafaring, I could at least sail boats; for in those Edwardian days, in spite of ankle-length skirts and ludicrous headgear, women had already proved themselves to be capable helmsmen and efficient hands in small craft.

The first step in my aquatic dedication had now to be taken; and at my baptism in the font of Christ Church, Lancaster Gate, my maternal grandfather, who performed the ceremony, named me after three of the best-known and most successful racing-yachts of the summer in which I was born. These names, fortunately for me, were considerably more suitable and euphonious than many of those in use today; and on the principle that there is nothing like starting a child off in the way she should go, I was taken for my first sail at the age of six weeks, propped up in a corner of the cockpit of a small, half-decked centre-board boat on the Norfolk Broads. Family summer holidays were spent inevitably at some convenient sailing-ground; and when after his breakdown in health the doctors banished my father from his parish for a period of at least six months, he rented for the first three of them a house called Braganza, at St Mawes in Cornwall. Thither we migrated in the spring of 1909, accompanied by Nanny, a hamperful of house-linen, another of plate; the pianola, crated; and our terriers Scamp and Jack. And I am not at all sure that we did not take Elizabeth and Mrs Packer as well.

This kind of wholesale exodus was perfectly normal in those days when railway fares and freights were low. We

thought nothing of taking linen and plate for our annual
month by the sea or on the Broads; and since boats were an
indispensable part of any holiday to my father, our boats,
too, followed us across the railway systems of England and
back again.

The metamorphosis from the baking brick desert of Poplar
to the green hills of Devon and Cornwall seemed scarcely less
magical and far more real than the transformation scene that
we watched each Christmas with such breathless wonder at
the Drury Lane pantomime. It might have been a different
planet: rolling countryside instead of factory chimneys; the
thick, white dust of the lanes rising in an ashen train from
beneath the carriage wheels, and the cropped, springy turf
of the headlands underfoot instead of the soiled town pavements; the delicious, unaccustomed smells of foliage, flowers,
earth and farmyards instead of the nauseating odours of
chemicals, fried fish-shops and poverty. Above all, the sea;
and it was during that long summer idyll of our stay at
Braganza that I achieved two accomplishments of major
significance in my education: I learned to swim, and to sail
a boat.

Braganza, as I remember it, was a large grey house standing high up on the hillside looking across the bay to Falmouth.
The garden was full of terraced flower-beds, steps flanked by
grey stone vases, and such exotic, semi-tropical plants as
eucalyptus trees and aloes. Far below, on the crawling blue
waters of the estuary, our beloved *Merry Dancer* floated, with
her own especial, incomparable and gull-like grace, at her
moorings.

I could never recall a day when we did not own *Merry
Dancer*, and it never occurred to me that there would ever
come a day when she would no longer be ours. We used to
promise never to part with her. 'Daddy, we'll be down to our
last crust of bread before we sell her!'

Such are the ardent, the ingenuous fidelities of youth. The

hard and dreary pressures of war, of economy, our inability to surmount the sheer physical obstacle of keeping her as she should be kept and sailing her as she should be sailed, forced my mother to sell her after my father's death. One could only bow to the inevitable. She was renowned for her sailing qualities, and coveted; there was a purchaser only too eager to lavish on her everything that we could not afford to give her: a bitter pill to swallow. Better so, than that she should moulder and rot in an odd corner of a boat-yard, gradually decaying, gradually falling apart until weeds and nettles began to grow through her timbers, and eventually someone chopped her up for firewood.

When my mother came to tell me that she had gone, I asked not to be told the buyer nor the price; and although I was then middle-aged, I gave myself up to a long storm of tears, as ridiculous as it was without reason: the absurd, impassioned, hopeless weeping of an ageing woman for the irrevocable passing of a symbol of youth.

I still feel that she is part of us and belongs to us, as though the mere changing hands of a sum of money could in no way loosen the bonds of such a close relationship. I allow myself the luxury of imagining that one day, before it is too late, I might even be able to buy her back. Meanwhile, I have never set eyes on her since; and I take good care not to frequent the waters where she is sailed by other hands than mine.

Merry Dancer was thirty-four feet in length overall; she had a maximum beam of six feet two inches—five and a half beams to length—and a draught of four feet. Her registered tonnage was four; she had about a ton and a half of lead on the bottom of her keel. Linton Hope designed her and she was built at Cowes at the beginning of the century. She was far ahead of her time and never looked old-fashioned. While in our possession she was variously rigged as a yawl for sea-sailing, a sliding-gunter-rigged sloop for the Broads, and finally as a Bermudan cutter, which suited her ideally for both sea and river.

These dry-as-dust technicalities convey nothing of her special personality and charm. Her long, low hull, painted black with a white boot-topping and red-brown anti-fouling, rested on the water with a kind of inevitability of rightness: the light sweep of her sheer flowed with the ease of a master-painter's brush-stroke, and the fine run of her stern had the natural poise of a bird floating on water. I have never set eyes on a more beautiful stem, the curve of her spoon bow springing from the water-line with a spirited dignity and a delicate grace.

In performance she was unequalled. I learnt to sail in her during that fabulous summer of 1909; I sailed her, off and on, for nearly forty years, and except for my father, no one is better qualified to speak of her than I am. She would turn on a sixpence, if you knew just how to throw her round; would pinch up into the wind if you wanted to weather a buoy or a point of land or a bend in a river, making the most of every puff, holding her ground when the breeze dropped light, clawing her way up to windward in a manner little short of miraculous, as though she knew very well just what was required of her. She had no best point of sailing; all points were equally her best. If I had a favourite, it was running with the wind just abaft the beam, when she would nuzzle her lee shoulder down into the water and go for her life, the sea boiling past down to leeward, a great stern-wave building up in a hillock under her weather quarter, and *Merry Dancer* herself purring and thrumming with satisfaction at her own cleverness. She was as sensitive in a river as she was staunch and dry at sea. She could tack like a fish up the narrowest of streams, for she held her way and would shoot her own length and more at the end of every board. In fact, as the old square-rigged sailorman used to say of his favourite ship, she could do everything but speak.

I have the clear sensation now of the feel of her tiller, grasped a little fearfully in a hand that was not yet quite large enough to hold it resolutely; of bracing one's short legs with no little difficulty against the lee-side of the cockpit as she heeled; of watching with an anxious eye fixed not, as when I was learning to steer, on some distant object—a rock, a house on shore, a beacon—but on the jib and the luff of the mainsail for the first sign of the tell-tale flutter. How gloriously she moved when she was sailing close-hauled on a wind! Her tanned sails were motionless as boards from leech to luff, from peak to foot, every inch of canvas working. She would heel over, settling herself down comfortably on her lee-side to exactly the right angle at which she could best match herself to beat the wind. The seething, foam-streaked waves rushed past below you, lipping the coaming of the cockpit in a hard puff; the cool, liquid, salty breath of the sea itself struck up at your face. When she had reached a certain speed, she would set up a deep humming in her rudder, as though crooning to herself with the sheer joy of doing superbly what she had been created to do well; and a steady vibration, a tremble of exaltation, was transmitted up from the water to the helmsman's hand on the tiller.

Sometimes in a stronger gust she would go over still further, burying the lee coaming, and the sea, drawing closer, would swish down the half-decking and splash into the cockpit itself.

'Luff!' ordered the calm voice of my father at the main-sheet. 'Remember what I told you. Always luff in the puffs!'

Scared and confused, I pushed the tiller away from me, but too hard and too far. Instantly she swooped up like a bird into the wind and jumped upright on an even keel, sails snapping, main-sheet blocks rattling furiously in the claws overhead and thumping on the after-deck, annoyed, you might have said, at being checked so clumsily in her swift passage.

'Now you've luffed up too much. Bear away again!'

Judgement came slowly when you were small, and the necessary concentration was not easy to maintain. She would be sailing along smoothly and well, and then all at once you would notice that she was not going so fast, that her angle of heel was gradually decreasing. The thrumming of the tiller had stopped; there was a sensation of faltering—your attention had been wandering and you had not observed that ominous fluttering of the jib. . . .

'Think what you're doing. You're starving her—sail her full!' the placid voice would say in a minatory tone; ashamed of the rebuke, you would stretch every faculty, nerve and muscle, for as long as you were allowed to keep the tiller, to the task of 'sailing her full'.

Every day we cruised about Carrick Roads, or up the Fal, or best of all, out to sea into the wide horizon of the English Channel, inviting us by its very emptiness to come and find what lay beyond. At the age of fourteen my father and two of his brothers had hired a boat, with a professional hand—who proved to be useless, for he rapidly drank himself insensible—and had sailed it all the way to France. I was never tired of hearing of this remarkable exploit, in which my father had been the moving spirit, and wished passionately that we might repeat it, especially when *Merry Dancer*, reaching the bar, began to feel the first of the swell riding in from outside. She would lift and dip to the waves with an exhilarating motion, at once smooth and buoyant. Her timbers creaked a little; you could feel them coming alive to the force of the sea.

Here was a big one, bearing down on us unhurried and relentless, its crest just toppling over in a curl of white. Up she flung, poised herself on the summit, dropped down with a crash, the foam splaying out in a great arc on either hand. The first bucketful of glittering spray flew over her weather-bow, travelled aft like silver shot and landed, stinging smartly, on your face. You put your tongue out and licked the drops: *real* sea-water from the open sea itself!

'Well done!' said my father. 'You're getting the hang of her now.'

Merry Dancer's crew consisted nominally of my sister and myself, augmented occasionally by Charlie, a local fisher-lad, who was supposed to keep our boats clean—we had a launch and an old pram dinghy as well—get *Merry Dancer* ready for hoisting in the morning and put her away, under supervision, at night. Now and again we would take him out with us, for it seemed a shame that he should have all the work and none of the pleasure; but Charlie had one serious handicap: he was a poor sailor.

His place on board when we were under way was aft, sitting on a small hatch-cover immediately forward of the mizzenmast. At times we noticed that Charlie was rather quiet, but it never occurred to us that he, born and bred to the sea, could be feeling unwell until there came a day when, the breeze falling light, the sun being hot and the swell what is graphically described as oily, the deplorable commotion of Charlie being sick all over the after-deck startled us out of our complacency. Poor Charlie! He was overcome with shame and embarrassment, more especially since my sister and I—the landlubbers, the Cockneys—appeared to be quite impervious to the motion. Not unnaturally, we prided ourselves on our immunity, boasted of it and rubbed it in to the humiliated Charlie.

Pride goeth before a fall. On calm days, light weather days, usually when running before the wind, we children liked to sit side by side on the counter, dangling our legs over the stern and trailing our feet in the sea. My father forbade us to do this; he declared that it stopped our way, but I fancy his real reason was a fear that we might fall overboard unnoticed while his attention was held by tiller and sheet.

We were sailing idly about off-shore on one of those blazing hot days of which there seem to have been so many in those bygone summers. The sun, shining out of a cloudless sky, had 'killed the wind', but a long swell was coming in from the Atlantic, although the surface of the sea was glassy, and the main boom banged wilfully to and fro over our heads. My sister and I slid cautiously aft and lowered our feet into the cool water. It was delicious; it flowed refreshingly round our hot ankles as the counter rose and fell rhythmically to the swell; you could gaze far down into the clear green depths, where all sorts of interesting objects, seaweed, cuttle-fish bones, and starfish swam past in the fascinating underwater world.

My father looked round and ordered us back into the cockpit. We refused to budge, how unwisely we were to discover all too soon; for in the sort of voice that we knew allowed of no further defiance we were condemned to the cabin—a dreaded punishment. My father shut the cabin-doors, bolted them, and pulled the sliding-hatch securely over all: we were immured in hot, musty gloom.

Merry Dancer's cabin, it must be admitted, was neither spacious nor comfortable. There were two very low seats furnished with hard, flat cushions, upon which you sat with your knees up to your chin; two lockers containing enamel mugs and thick glass tumblers; two net-racks in which were kept spare charts, fishing-lines, and burgee-sticks. The cabin of the *Dulcibella*, which so appalled Carruthers by its inadequacy, would have appeared palatial by comparison, although mercifully we did not have to contend with a centre-board case. (In our family *The Riddle of the Sands* attained the status of a sort of secular Bible; we read it constantly with devotion and could recite whole passages by heart.) Beneath our feet the bilge-water gurgled and splashed, scarcely veiled by wooden gratings which were easily removable so that we could cool the ginger-beer bottles down there or get at the pump-intake when it became choked. At its forward end, where the cabin-roof came down so low that even I could not sit upright, there hung a curtain of bright red Turkey twill, decently clothing the nakedness of the mast tabernacle and hiding the unsightly interior of the forward locker—grandly known as the forecastle—where the sail-covers and spare jibs were stored. The place was quite inadequately lit by four tiny oval scuttles of greenish glass, invariably dirty, through which one saw little save a lee-runner and a portion of undulating sea moving past in alarming proximity. There was a strong smell of stagnant salt-water, mildew, stale varnish and rust. To make matters worse, we had put out lines for mackerel on the previous day, and the decaying bait added its lively odour to the rest.

We sat miserably in the stuffy heat and the dim light filtering through the slats of the cabin-doors and the little scuttles. Overhead we could hear canvas thrashing, ropes and blocks flailing the cabin-roof: evidently the wind had freshened, we had gone about and were beating back to our moorings. Each time we tacked my head went round and—there was no denying it—I began to feel sick; my sister, too, admitted that she felt distinctly queasy. I grew tearful, and we exhausted ourselves rattling at the door-handle and begging to be let out. But my father was adamant; we were to learn, once and for all, the lesson that we must not dangle our legs over the stern.

By the time we got home, we were extremely subdued. Even the fresh air while we stowed the sails and rowed ashore failed to revive us. At tea I had to refuse my favourite Cornish splits and cream. All very well for my mother to try and comfort me with tales of Nelson, for Nanny to mutter darkly that 'your father had been too hard on you'; lying on a singularly knobbly red plush sofa, my face to the wall so that I should not have to endure watching the others at tea, I was preoccupied with the gravity of this new development. Not by one hair's-breadth had it affected my resolution to become a sailor; but I had serious doubts as to whether it might not impair my efficiency. There were no two ways about it; I was now on exactly the same level as Charlie: I had been seasick!

But to Charlie the slow-witted, the simple fisher-lad, it is not at all improbable that we owe our lives. Coming back from an afternoon sail, the wind fell away to a flat calm, and *Merry Dancer*, caught by the ebb-tide, began to drift out to sea stern-first into the evening mists that lay beyond the bar. By nightfall we were anchored in thick fog, hoping that we were well inside the steamer-lanes. I cannot recall that I was frightened; my father was calm, cheerful, and reassuring as ever; and in the unlikely event that he would need moral support, another man, a sailing-friend who happened to be staying with us, was in the party.

At first I thought it all a great adventure; but then I grew cold, sleepy and hungry, and began to wish that I were back in my comfortable bed in the night-nursery at Braganza. Occasionally we heard the regular thumping of a ship's propeller, but it never occurred to me that we might be in danger. Once this pounding noise came very near indeed, although there was nothing to be seen in the dense, unbroken ring of fog all round us. My father and the sailing-friend climbed out on deck, one forward and the other aft, shouting at the tops of their voices. The thrashing sound grew suddenly loud, and startlingly out of the thickness there materialised the straight black cut-water of a ship with two white bow-waves curling like moustaches on either side. She missed us quite comfortably by our own length at least; her hull slid rapidly by, as high as a cliff, although I don't suppose she was larger than 2,000 tons or so. She must have been steaming a great deal too fast, and I cannot remember that she was blowing her whistle. The water all round us boiled and seethed alarmingly, and for a long time after she had disappeared we were rolling wildly in her wake.

So far as I was concerned, minutes or hours may have passed

before we heard a faint, familiar chugging. We all bawled and shouted with desperate energy; and as though led to us unerringly, there emerged from the darkness the well-known varnished bow bearing the two small painted burgees of the Royal Cruising Club: the bow of our own launch, piloted by none other than the diffident Charlie. Happening to see *Merry Dancer* retreating rapidly stern-first out to sea at sunset, Charlie had braced himself up for the considerable ordeal of searching for us after dark, in dense fog, and in charge of a launch which only seldom had he been allowed to drive: an achievement which, for all his familiarity with the local coast-line, demanded no small amount of pluck.

At the end of the long tow home—for we had dragged, or drifted, a good deal further out to sea than we had thought— my mother was waiting for us at the water-side steps, holding a lantern over her head like a character from *The Wreckers*. For the first time in my life I perceived that she was genuinely angry with my father; and it was then that I heard her use to him a phrase of which the significance escaped me: 'One day the pitcher will go too often to the well!' What on earth could it mean?

My father wished me to be quite fearless on the water, for he maintained that people were only nervous in boats because they could not swim and therefore were terrified of falling overboard; so that summer I learnt to swim by the elementary process of being thrown into the sea from the deck of *Merry Dancer*. Not for me any half-measures such as having my chin held up in shallow water, nor any unreliable fripperies, such as 'water-wings'. With *Merry Dancer* standing well off the land towards the open sea, there would be an apprehensive and chilly moment on deck while a bight of the main halyard was made fast round my middle. Then, screaming with panic, I was thrown mercilessly over the side, sympathising in my extremity with the 'timorous mortals' of the hymn, who 'start and shrink and fear to launch away'.

I soon discovered that I did not sink and splashed about with confidence, like a puppy. In any case, I had the halyard to hang on by, and if my father saw that I was being towed too fast through the water, he would shake up into the wind. After ten minutes or so, I would be hauled back on board, a drowned rat of a child; but I no longer feared deep water, and clearly, since I had determined that my life was to be spent at sea, swimming and diving were accomplishments that I must acquire.

As I grew older, this question of going to sea began to cause me a good deal of worry. I was hopelessly committed, already deeply convinced, like Captain McWhirr of the steamer *Nan-Shan*, of the infinite inferiority of the land upon which I was still unfortunately compelled to live. The ineffably smooth, gliding motion of a vessel over the surface of the sea, the sense of immense freedom once you were afloat— what was to prevent you following those enticing horizons to the ends of the earth?—the happy circumstance of self-contained sufficiency experienced by any voyager however small his craft, his mobile world independent of the shore: every aspect of the life on water, as I then knew it, struck me as eminently desirable and immeasurably preferable to the life on land. But I was growing uneasily aware, thanks to voluminous reading and persistent questioning of our sea-faring acquaintances, that I had been born a generation too late. Thirty or forty years earlier, and I could have married a sea-captain and spent the rest of my life happily sailing round the world with him, like Captain and Mrs Lowe of the tea-clipper *N. B. Palmer*.

Unfortunately, it seemed to be getting more and more rare for ships' captains to take their wives to sea with them, at any rate in the British Merchant Service. Thanks to the tiresome reliability of steam, voyages now lasted for weeks, whereas formerly they had taken an unspecified number of months; steamers ran to a schedule with the vexing regularity of a railway time-table; there was really no excuse at all for a man to take his wife with him in these enlightened days of twentieth-century progress.

Had I but known it, I had also been born a generation too early. Twenty or thirty years later and I should have been besieging the offices of shipping companies with applications for a job as a sea-going stenographer—surely one of the most attractive occupations for any young woman with an insatiable desire to wander. But in those early decades of the new century it seemed to be increasingly difficult for a female to go to sea in any other role than that of stewardess, which failed to appeal to me as a congenial occupation.

In the meantime I attempted to pursue a vaguely nautical curriculum, struggling manfully with intractable cord, rope and wire to learn the crafts of knotting, splicing and serving so essential to good seamanship, despising dolls, party-frocks and lessons in embroidery as deplorably effeminate, and glorying in my holiday rig of sailor's cap, fisherman's jersey, and a cut-down pair of my father's rowing-shorts. Even during the winter months in Poplar I insisted on wearing boys' boots with little metal clips instead of eyelet holes for the laces; and I refused categorically to endure the detestable bonnets tied under the chin with satin bows, which were then the accepted headgear for little girls, as for old ladies. Encouraged by my father, I clung obstinately to the sailor's cap, complete with a real tally-ribbon printed in gold letters with the proud legend: H.M.S. BRITANNIA.

These magic words once served me a very good turn in an awkward situation. On February 1st, 1911, the very last man-of-war to be built on the Thames, H.M.S. *Thunderer*, was to be launched; and most suitably attired in jersey and skirt, dark-blue reefer jacket and my *Britannia* cap, I accompanied my father to the ceremony.

As an occasion it was at once historic and mournful. The Thames Ironworks would be closing down after this final 'job' had left the ways, and henceforth the shipbuilding industry would belong entirely to the north. Naturally, I understood little of the sadness of the breaking of a long tradition, the ending of an era that had lasted for centuries on Thames-side. A thin, wasted, grey old man, sitting in a bath-chair and swathed in rugs, spoke to us in quavering tones from a platform inside a marquee. He seemed much moved by what he had to say, and at times scarcely able to continue. I found the speech-making tedious, but I was at once bewildered and thrilled by the gigantic stem of the ship towering above us. The tiny forms of men peered down at us over her bow; ceremonial bunting fluttered from a grove of scaffolding; and a knot of workmen crouched under her keel ready to knock out the dog-shores at the moment of launching.

That moment, when it arrived, brought a sensation of incredulity as the huge bulk, apparently immovable as our church, began to slide away from us down the slips, slowly at first, and then with an increasing urgency as though straining to leave the alien land for the broad pathway of the River that would lead her to the sea. The clamour, the sudden burst of cheering, the deep thundering of the ship herself over the ways, the roar and surge of water as a turbulent wave, tossing debris on its crest, rushed back towards us in the wake of the ship, were both frightening and emboldening. My father was waving his hat and cheering heartily. I tried to do the same, but no sound would come for the strange choking sensation in my throat.

The *Thunderer*, floating triumphantly out in the stream, was transformed; one saw her as she was meant to be, come to life and handsome on the element for which she was intended. She curtseyed a little to us, as though thanking us for our interest in her start in the world; then the tugs got hold of her and pushed and pulled her out of sight.

Meanwhile I, quite witless and confused with excitement, realised that I had lost my father. We had become separated in the crowd, and I found myself groping with increasing dismay among a forest of unfamiliar legs and strange over-coats. I had always been told by Nanny and my parents that, if ever I got lost, there was not the slightest need for panic. Look about for a policeman, they said, tell him who you are, and where you live, and all will be well. But here there seemed to be no policemen, and I burst into tears.

Evidently alarmed at my distress, a man with a clean-shaven face, blue eyes, very kind and much crinkled at the corners, bent down and asked if he could be of any help. I explained that I had lost my father. Was that all? Nothing could be easier, it appeared, than to put the matter right. I was lifted up and settled firmly on the stranger's shoulder.

'Hang on tight and have a good look round,' I was com-manded reassuringly. 'He can't be far away—we'll find him all right!'

I was greatly comforted, and doing as I had been bidden, soon saw my father in the distance, searching just as anxiously for me. When I had been safely handed over, my father thanked the stranger warmly for his kindness.

'A pleasure, sir,' he declared. 'You see, I was in H.M.S. *Britannia* myself, so in a manner of speaking, your daughter and I are old shipmates!'

It amused my father to foster my distaste for feminine softness, just as he liked to encourage my passion for every-thing connected with the sea; and one of my ambitions was to crew him as a jib-sheethand, just as soon as I was big enough, strong enough, and heavy enough, in his famous half-rater *Atalanta*, which he raced with consistent success on the Thames at Teddington and Bourne End.

This type of craft, a racing-machine pure and simple, was aptly described as a skimming-dish. Incredibly light and fragile for their size, they were built of three-eighths of an inch planking, so that if anyone unversed in their ways stepped incautiously upon their decks, they were very liable to go crashing through. It was necessary to move about on board with cat-like delicacy; any sudden, unpremeditated action could be disastrous. I dare say they would look primitive enough to the racing enthusiast of today with his complicated array of winches, tramways, stretchers, and other modern aids to sailing. A jamming cleat and patent roller-reefing gear were considered the height of ingenuity then, and *Atalanta's* sail-plan would be dismissed as ridiculously archaic now, for the whole frail structure was driven through—and at times over—the water by an enormous area of canvas. In anything of a blow they capsized easily; nothing was thought of it, the crew scrambling out over the weather gunwale with remarkable agility to right their craft by standing up to their waists in water on the submerged centre-board.

My father was a superlative helmsman and profoundly practised in the art of racing small boats, but not all the *expertise* in the world could keep the light, over-canvassed craft going in a real hard blow without the aid of sufficient human ballast. Weight was essential; but long before I could qualify as crew, in fact as soon as I could steer a boat reliably, my father found a useful role for me.

At the beginning of each racing season *Atalanta* and three or four other half-raters had to be towed upstream by our sturdy launch *Tegumai* from Teddington, where they had been laid up for the winter, to Bourne End for the Easter-tide regattas. Each boat required a helmsman, and out of consideration for my age, I would be put in the sternmost boat where there was least to do. It was largely a matter of concentration on the steering, for too much veering about from side to side hampered the tow. Above all, there was the business of the locks; and it was here that my anxieties began.

As *Tegumai* slackened speed, it was necessary to run forward, take in the slack of the tow-line and prepare to fend-off, for the light-weight craft overran each other easily. And if the lock-keeper happened to be slow in opening his gates, or had a lockful of water to empty, trouble might develop. It was comparatively simple going upstream in spring when the flow of the river tended to keep the boats strung out, but coming downstream in early autumn was a different matter: the boats drifted quickly down upon each other and worse still, upon the launch; and there was always the drag of the weir. Its roar would frighten the life out of me, when the river was high and a great deal of water coming down; I would imagine myself sliding despairingly towards that steely rim beyond which boughs, driftwood, and weeds disappeared in a cloud of spray and with relentless ease.

More often than not the lock-gates would open in the nick of time and the little convoy would enter cautiously the dank and frightening cavern of the lock. As the last boat of the string I had to look sharp, for as soon as my stern was inside the gates would close and the lock-keeper would open his sluices at the upstream end. At this juncture you had to do several things at once: steer towards the side of the lock, fend-off, make sure that your tow-line did not foul anyone else's rudder or—worst crime in the calendar—*Tegumai's* propeller; and get out your boat-hook and fasten it securely through a link of one of the long iron chains hanging down the sides of the lock. There was nothing for it then but to hang on like grim death as the swirl of the sluice-water threatened to bang the fragile hulls together; scrabbling for a hold on the slimy walls, praying that you would not let go the chain, and fending-off desperately as the turbulent inflow bubbled round you.

Once risen to the surface, the opening lock-gates revealed a new vista of tranquil Thames spread invitingly ahead. One final prod of the boat-hook to get your stern clear of the gates, and you could settle down again at the tiller for the next long reach. In fine weather it was a day as enjoyable and exciting as you could wish, with the sun glinting on the water and the new varnish of the boats, and the ever-changing scenery of the banks to watch. There would be a strong feeling of spring in the air, of something stirring from winter's sleep, of long fine days ahead; and the boats themselves, jostling each other as though impatient to be off, sleek, glossy, chestnut-brown and mettlesome, were not unlike a string of spirited racehorses setting off for a morning gallop.

Year after year my father added to the collection of silver rose-bowls, cream-jugs, goblets and tankards in the glass-fronted cases in the study. *Atalanta* became crack-boat on the River, securing such sought-after trophies as the Braganza Cup and the Queen's Challenge Cup, which last my father won outright. In fact, on looking back, it seems that I was never disappointed, that *Atalanta* always won; but perhaps the Spectacles of Proportion have become clouded with the warmth of Filial Devotion and rose-tinted with the patina of Time: I have forgotten that there were occasions when *Atalanta* did not win!

People, it seemed, were divided quite arbitrarily into two categories. Either you were born with a natural aversion to being in, on, or by the water that was almost impossible to overcome, however gallantly you might try—like my mother, who felt sick walking on a pier; or you belonged whole-heartedly and irrevocably—like my father and myself—to that affinity of persons who were drawn with the unfailing certitude of a steel splinter attracted by a magnet, to the sea and ships, boats and water.

I would reflect upon this curious and recently-discovered truth during the long, dark London winter, when the sea and sailing were very far away and months must pass before my hand would grasp *Merry Dancer's* tiller once again. At night I slept with a piece of tarred twine under my pillow.

8. Edwardian Nursery

My sister, on seeing me for the first time, suggested cautiously to my father, in whose arms I was being displayed to her, that the only really satisfactory answer to the problem of my unfortunate arrival was to throw me out of the window. I was then a week old; and since she had enjoyed a five years' monopoly of the Lancaster Gate nursery, her reaction was perfectly understandable.

In time she became reconciled to my continued existence, although the disparity in our ages was too great ever to be overlooked entirely, and her departure for boarding-school merely emphasised the gap between us. Before we left Poplar she had reached her teens, and had become involved in such mature and awe-inspiring activities as taking 'exams', attending dancing-classes and learning to play the piano. For this last she had a genuine talent. Languishing in the nursery, I would listen to her practising by the hour on the grand piano in the drawing-room, while I longed for the music to stop so that she might come upstairs again.

During the holidays we would amuse ourselves together

amicably enough, performing endless dramas, with the aid of
the 'dressing-up box', in which she was usually a queen or
princess, and I a slave or courtier. She liked also to occupy
herself with my dolls, in which I took no interest whatsoever.
Occasionally we fought, as a rule over possessions—the
Forsyte tendency again!—impassioned battles in which her
superior size and weight would tell, until Nanny, sharp-
tongued with vexation, would launch herself between the
two contestants, subduing our naughty rages with slaps and
admonitions.

Nevertheless, I was normally anxious to placate my sister,
for her goodwill was of importance to me; she was, with one
exception, my only playfellow; and when the age-long months
of term began I felt very sorry for myself, a solitary child
surrounded by swarms of children with whom, as I understood by now, I was not allowed to mix—save for Maggie
Saunders, who became the only friend I ever had in Poplar
of my own generation.

Her father was a guard on the railway: that is to say, in the
top stratum of Poplar society. He was also a pillar of our
church, and the Vicar's Warden for much of my father's nine
years' incumbency. Mr Saunders was immensely dark and
very dignified; he had a long, melancholy, sallow face, drooping moustaches and a faintly Oriental aspect. Maggie, small-
boned and dark-eyed, was a bright, clever child who came to
tea with me as often as my mother permitted me to ask her.
I expected her to arrive as soon after two o'clock as she could
and stay until my bedtime at six, that being my idea of the
proper duration of an afternoon tea-party; and I would look
out anxiously for the small figure of Maggie, always very
demure and neat, hurrying up St Leonard's Road.

Our pastimes would seem both dull and ingenuous to a
modern child: such simple-minded games as 'Hunt the Slipper';
dressing-up; sticking coloured scraps in a scrapbook; or
listening solemnly to a gramophone with a large crimson

horn for which I possessed a record of 'The Blessed City' to be played on Sundays, and one of 'The Toreador's Song' for week-day consumption only.

On occasion Maggie helped me with the exciting but monumental task of cooking and eating a full two-course dinner on a miniature cooking-stove, fuelled by methylated spirit, which I infinitely preferred to the dolls, although Maggie, like my sister, was tiresomely enthusiastic over them, exclaiming rapturously over their beautiful, hand-made trousseaux with which I had never bothered to experiment.

Our menu was usually stew, and the cutting-up of meat and vegetables into small enough quantities to go into the minute saucepans occupied us for hours. With an equal lack of inventiveness, the sweet was invariably jam-tart, its pastry somewhat leaden in texture and nearly grey in colour from much handling. Unfortunately, by the time all was ready the two cooks, hot, exhausted, and covered with smuts, were almost too jaded to eat the meal. It would be spirited away tactfully by Nanny, who must have dreaded the mess we made, for we were exempt from the horrors of washing-up: a serious error in training which I have since regretted.

Having salved our consciences by consuming a few per-functory mouthfuls, we were only too thankful to sit up to the table for a good nursery tea: a foretaste of the lesson one had to learn so hardly in later life, that food prepared by oneself is never so palatable as that prepared by others!

Far more enjoyable than having Maggie to tea was going to tea with Maggie. In fact, I doubt whether I should have invited Maggie to the Vicarage at all if I had not early recog-nised the *quid pro quo* principles of established hospitality: a tea-party for a tea-party. With her own housework to do, Maggie's mother naturally did not want us there so early as two o'clock; we would be bidden for four, and the hours after lunch would pass with fantastic slowness, but in happy anticipation, until it was time to be dressed in a tidy frock and to set forth, with Nanny, for Maggie's home.

It was the most ordinary house in an ordinary side-street—a turning to the right off St Leonard's Road and quite close to South Bromley Station—but you could tell at once what sort of people lived there, for the front-door was neatly painted and the doorstep well scrubbed and 'stoned'. Once inside, you were conscious of spotless cleanliness, despite the smallness of the rooms and the worn condition of much of the furniture. Nanny used to say that we could eat our dinners off the floor, a remark which puzzled me for years. Not that I bothered my head about such things; I was plainly and unashamedly interested in the delicious smell of baking that filled the house; and could barely restrain my impatience for the moment when tea was announced to be ready, and we sat down at a large table spread with a very white cloth and literally covered with plates of the most inviting food.

Mrs Saunders was a Scotswoman, and she had lost none of the skills of Scots cooking through her translation to East London. It was here that I made the acquaintance of such northern delicacies as drop scones, Scotch pancakes, oatcakes, buckwheat cakes, soda-cake, gingerbread in rich, dark, treacly slabs, and many more. It was a point of honour—with me, at any rate—to eat something from every plate, from the obligatory bread and butter through every variety of 'tea-bread' to the last, slowly-consumed morsel of cake. Replete to the limit of discomfort, I would be taken home by Nanny along the foggy, gaslit streets—St Michael's clock-face hanging high like a murky harvest moon in the smoky haze overhead —vaguely wishing that we could have such good things to eat at home.

Alas! At the Vicarage our culinary arrangements were in the hands of Mrs Packer, about whom Nanny used to make the perennial joke, which I thought excruciatingly funny, that whatever else Mrs Packer might pack, it was not our stomachs.

I seldom saw this dismal personage, for I was not supposed to go into the kitchen. Very rarely I would accompany my mother there after breakfast, when she discharged the tedious daily rite of 'doing the orders'. The kitchen is usually the hub of the house to a child, the G.H.Q., as it were, of everything to do with food. The Poplar kitchen was sunny, and in summer-time overheated by an enormous Eagle range, the size of half a motor car. I enjoyed watching my mother write down what we were going to have to eat with a squeaky pencil on a large slate; but in reality I felt that I was on hostile ground, guilty of a faint disloyalty towards Nanny: the traditional warfare between nursery and kitchen was fought punctiliously, if without rancour, at the Vicarage. Mrs Packer, I remarked, made few helpful contributions to the planning of our menus. She would stand respectfully at the far side of the kitchen-table, an elderly woman with scanty greying hair screwed into a knot at the back of her head. (My father used to observe, until categorically forbidden to do so by my mother, that it was small wonder she had so little hair on her head when such a lot of it found its way into our food.) She had a habit of clapping her hand to her mouth whenever she smiled to hide her excruciatingly bad teeth. I imagine she would have had difficulty in finding employment anywhere else than in a slum vicarage with my long-suffering mother: her gift for spoiling food was quite extraordinary. Over the years that she was with us at Poplar—and I cannot recall another cook—she produced with unfailing regularity from the Eagle range a succession of flavourless stews, watery minces, inedible puddings, overdone joints, soggy cakes with the minimum of currants, and pastry scarcely less leaden than mine. Incredible though it may seem, her cooking never improved; nevertheless, she remained with us, and for that alone my poor mother must have been grateful, since she had the greatest difficulty in persuading any domestic staff at all to stay in such a locality as Poplar.

Our house-parlourmaid, Elizabeth Tyler, was a native of Bow. For years I remained firmly convinced of the connection between Elizabeth and a public-house in the neighbourhood called 'The Tiler's Arms'. It never occurred to me to mention it to Elizabeth herself, and I was genuinely surprised to discover eventually that the name had a different connotation. Children, I fancy, commonly adopt this method of worrying out for themselves the things that puzzle them, and contenting themselves with their own solution. Thus I accepted unquestioningly the private explanation that 'sundry places' as mentioned in the Book of Common Prayer referred to deserts, and 'divers orders' to the deep-sea divers such as I saw working in the Docks. As for the reference in the Collect for Peace to 'service' being 'perfect freedom', I could not see how any *church* service could be so described, since one had to exercise the most rigid self-control in order to sit still while it lasted!

Elizabeth was indeed a true Cockney, tough, sharp-tongued, hard-working, robust and independent. Even when dressed up in her 'afternoon blacks' with a clean, crackling apron tied round her sturdy waist, she never managed to look smart. She objected to wearing a cap, and often earned my shocked disapproval by leaving it off for no apparent reason. She was, I suspect, a Socialist in embryo, for I frequently overheard her making remarks to Mrs Packer about her equality with 'them in the room'—a mystifying saying, for I had no idea about whom she was talking. For all that, I think she was fond of us in her undemonstrative way, although my mother often sighed over her intransigence. She had a hot temper, too, and there would be 'words' with Nanny, usually over my meals, for inevitably Elizabeth took sides with Mrs Packer.

Everything about Elizabeth was large, strong and plain. She was a large-boned woman; she had a large face in which every feature was proportionate, excepting her eyes which were small and pale with sandy lashes. It seemed scarcely credible that any woman should be so little favoured by the grace of nature; but perhaps I am wrong even in that, for she had very large, strong, perfect teeth, white and square, with which she bit and crunched easily the hardest substances, such as nuts, toffee, lump sugar and coconut-meat. At least she had no illusions about her appearance, wasted no money on creams or lotions, and would have rejected cosmetics scornfully as 'not respectable'.

'I was behind the door when God was dishin' out the good looks,' she would say with her strong, rasping Cockney humour, 'so I've been pushin' meself forward ever since!'

'Face-cream!' she would exclaim ironically. 'Plain yellow soap's good enough for the kitchen-table—and me face!'

There was so little of the feminine about Elizabeth, and she was so reticent in her replies to my constant questioning about her young man, in whom I was deeply interested, that he may well have been hypothetical. But on her Sundays off, dressed in a 'costume' of neat blue cloth, her hair puffed out becomingly on either side of the coarse-skinned, angular face, beneath a large straw hat trimmed with a rakish 'ruche' or quill, she would assume a faintly dashing aspect. She was as ebulliently cheerful as she was capable, and would throw back her head and laugh loud and long—generally at her own sallies—with a great display of pink gums and those large white teeth. But once, tiptoeing into the forbidden regions of the kitchen, I found her sitting at the table and crying noisily. I was utterly nonplussed at coming upon the great, bouncing, rugged creature in an attitude of collapse, snivelling and sobbing, her eyes red and swollen. It was the first time I had witnessed open adult grief. I burst into tears myself out of sheer sympathy; but Elizabeth would never let me know what private tragedy of the heart, or the purse, or wounded vanity, had brought about this disintegration of her usual robust morale.

If I am to round off satisfactorily this little gallery of

domestic portraits, the largest canvas of all must be reserved for Nanny. Indeed, the gallery would be incomplete without her; even after half a century the small, neat, devoted figure stands out most clearly in the fading light of that half-forgotten Poplar landscape.

Wrestling with the gargantuan labours of the parish, my parents gave what time they could spare to me, and it was generous enough; but inevitably I was thrown much on Nanny's hands and spent the greater part of my waking day with her. Mercifully, I can still use the present tense when speaking of her, for, retired and drawing a pension, she is enjoying the well-deserved fruits of her labours. Nanny is an orphan, her parentage obscure. She was, in fact, almost the traditional foundling, discovered on the doorstep, a note pinned to her shawl. Left in the care of a convent, she was so weak from under-feeding and consequent rickets that she was unable until the age of three to do anything but crawl about the floor. Nevertheless, the handicapped body was inhabited by an indomitable spirit; and the Sister of Mercy who looked after her from infancy was able to report that she was 'full of fun and ready for play at any time'.

Whatever her origins, she received from somewhere a nature at once courageous and humble, selfless and independent. Like all the best nannies, she is typical; she has inherited—or evolved for herself—the classic gift of suitable repartee, the traditional nursery manner, all Olympian calm and omnipotence. She can still subdue me, in my own house, with a phrase. Only the other day I was rash enough to tease her about her aversion to fresh fruit, considered an indispensable item of the modern diet.

'I've got on well enough without it for nearly eighty years,' observed Nanny in a dry, flat, annihilating tone, raising her eyebrows disapprovingly and staring at some point above my head with a devastating effect.

Nanny was twenty-six years old when she came to my

mother in Lancaster Gate. Trained by the convent for domestic service, and launched on her career as an under-housemaid at the age of seventeen and a wage of twelve pounds per annum, she soon discovered that children appealed to her considerably more than brooms and brushes, without taking into account the fact that nannies get higher pay than housemaids. So she decided, with a characteristic mixture of prudence and initiative, to take up children's nursing. Not for her a long, expensive training, a stylish uniform and a drawerful of diplomas. She studied carefully a few books on the care of infants; for the rest, she used her common sense. Combined with her undoubted flair for handling children, it seems to have been an adequate preparation, for all her babies, of whom I was but the first of a long line, have flourished.

With a calm outward demeanour but no little inward trepidation, she 'took me from the month', wondering if she would last as long; accompanied us to Poplar and remained with us until 1913, when my mother, with real regret and deep misgiving, decided that she must retrench. Nanny was obliged to leave us; and I was inconsolable for months.

Little about Nanny seems to have changed since those distant days of serenity and peace—except that I have grown tall, and she, perhaps, has shrunk, as one does with age, and consequently only reaches now to just above my elbow. In appearance, she was never anything above the ordinary; in fact, Nanny would be the first to describe herself as 'not much to look at'. But if nature has not been kind to her, Providence has been generous. Battling valiantly through life against successive disappointments and difficulties, and above all, entirely on her own, Nanny has brought triumphantly with her along that uphill road an irrepressible sense of fun, a true humility, the lasting affection of old friends and a religious faith, as deep as it is simple, that has been and ever will be, her firmest standby. And all this can be read in her face, kindly, humorous, a little apple-wrinkled now, but to me still the same: the familiar, comforting, much-loved face that was of such prime importance in my infant world.

I ran to her when I was in trouble, I turned to her in all my many problems. On her 'days off' I felt strange, lonely, and always faintly apprehensive for fear she might never come back at all. (Oh, the blessed relief of waking up next morning to see, in the dim light of dawn, the reassuring hump of Nanny's sleeping form in the other bed!) Indeed, I suffered from a perpetual lurking suspicion that she was going to be taken away from me altogether; and on the rare occasions when a trained nurse had to be engaged, I would only endure her attentions because I was aware of Nanny hovering in the background.

An experience far more alarming than congestion of the lungs, when I believed Nanny lost to me for ever, occurred when my tonsils had to be removed. My grandfather believed firmly in sparing no expense where health was involved, and despite the simplicity of the operation, he insisted that an eminent surgeon, accompanied by his own anæsthetist, should drive down from London to perform it at my grandparents' house in Kent.

Naturally, I was not warned of this ordeal beforehand, and one day, without a word of explanation, I was kept in bed and given hardly any breakfast. Since I felt perfectly well, I became frightened and suspicious, waiting miserably upon events while I wondered what on earth they could be going to do to me. Even Nanny, although fondly comforting, would not enlighten me; and one of my cousins added to my growing terror by putting her head round the door to gloat sadistically over my plight.

'I *am* sorry for you!' she remarked suggestively, and disappeared.

By the time two strange men and a nurse had arrived, addressing me with a horrible false heartiness and bringing with them an unpleasant piece of apparatus, I was in much the same state of near-panic as a bullock being driven to the *abattoir* when he first scents the blood of his unfortunate predecessors. Worst of all, everyone, including Nanny, was sent out of the room; and when the sinister trio gathered closely round my bed, I was prepared for any ghastly fate.

'Do you like scent?' the younger man inquired fatuously, while the elder, venerable, grey-haired, and attired, I fancy, in a morning coat, beamed ghoulishly at his elbow.

Strictly on the defensive, I replied with caution: 'Only Cherry Blossom,' having bought a bottle of this innocuous perfume at the Church Bazaar.

'Then here's something very much nicer!' exclaimed the anæsthetist, coming out in his true colours by clapping over my face a metal mask rather like a large coffee-strainer, on to which he shook something out of a bottle.

The gloves were off now with a vengeance. I was choking, I was being murdered. 'Nanny! Nanny!' I yelled despairingly. Had I but known it, Nanny was listening outside the door, weeping bitterly. I kicked and fought and used all the words I heard on the Poplar trams, which I knew were very wicked. The nurse attempted to hold my legs, but with a final effort, I kicked her violently in the stomach. . . . Afterwards, during convalescence, I grew comparatively fond of her, and she, strange to relate, of me; but the first word I uttered on my return to consciousness, before being extremely sick into a basin, was a feeble 'Nanny!'

Nanny grew to love Poplar and made many friends there. From time to time we paid them visits, which made a welcome interruption in the monotony of our daily walks. There was an excitable lady who seemed quite unable to stop talking, who would tell our fortunes by cards, tea-leaves, or palmistry, according to your fancy. In a dismal basement-kitchen lived a mournful person who took in washing, and whose husband had a deplorable habit of getting drunk on Saturday nights and pelting her with her own flat-irons. I am not at all sure that he did not also beat her—a normal occurrence in Poplar, regarded as reprehensible, but exciting no special comment. We would be expected to commiserate, even to examine the bruises; and while the recital of her dreary griefs droned on, punctuated by Nanny remarking: 'Fancy!' or 'Tut-tut!' at suitable moments, I would sit in the window, gazing up entranced at the passing legs and feet seen from this unusual angle: the shapeless, broken boots of the down-and-outs, the thick-soled, heavy boots of workmen, the more stylish shoes of the rent-collector and the insurance agent; the carpet-slippers, slit open to relieve a painful bunion, of old women creeping to the pub for a jug of supper-beer.

Here, too, with a suitable shade of hesitation, Nanny would accept 'just a cup of tea, then—so refreshing!' The kettle would sing softly on the shining black range, hot cinders fell out with a crash, too near for comfort to the old, sleeping tabby-cat curled up in a ball inside the polished fender. There was a smell of fresh ironing and fresh-made tea, superimposed on the rich, ancient aroma of a thousand meals, a hundred wash-days.

But my favourite of all was Louie, daughter of the church-cleaner at Nanny's chosen place of worship, St Frideswide's. Louie's was a poor home, permeated with something I had early learnt to recognise: a faint smell of damp, of ancient clothes, of ill-aired rooms, stale cooking and poor health. Not the pungent smell of real dirt and destitution, which penetrated to the Tumty Room, the Parish Hall and even to the Vicarage study; but the genuine odour of 'respectable' poverty, poverty kept, at the cost of unremitting and grinding struggle, just at bay—no more.

Louie was a young woman of about twenty-five, I suppose, and a cripple from birth. She was also desperately anæmic, her skin the waxen white of a Madonna lily, her lips as blood-less as milk. She had lovely sea-green eyes and clouds of the most glorious red hair of which she was passionately proud:

146

long, glossy and brilliant, despite her ill-health. She had narrow, delicate, bony hands, nearly transparent and veined in blue, with which she crocheted endlessly and exquisitely, anything from elaborate borders for altar-cloths to 'duchess-sets' for dressing-tables: it was her only means of contributing to the common exchequer. She was as thin as a lath, and the great, shiny, ugly black surgical boot without which I never saw her seemed like a hideous and cruelly heavy anchor dragging on the slight limbs and fragile body.

But nothing was allowed to weigh down her spirits. Louie was unchangingly gay and always made us welcome in the tiny kitchen where much of her life was spent, looking out over an iron railing to the drab houses opposite. In summer-time the room was often uncomfortably hot from the kitchen-stove; beads of sweat stood out on Louie's white forehead, and I could not understand why no one ever suggested opening the window. Louie would insist upon us staying to tea. Managing her crutches with a dexterity that seemed little short of miraculous to me, she would lay the table with a loaf of bread, some highly-coloured jam, and something that we never saw at home—a yellow pat of margarine.

Well-coached by Nanny, I knew that Louie's parents were too poor to buy butter, let alone cake, and that it was only good manners to eat up the food provided without comment, as though it were the best in the world. The meal was always merry, for Louie's cheerfulness was infectious. She and Nanny would chatter away, exchanging jokes and sallies at top Cockney speed, until Nanny's tears were rolling down her cheeks and she would gasp: 'Don't make me laugh any more!' If I did not always understand the humour, which was very largely concerned with the clergy and congregation of St Frideswide's, at least I could bask in the atmosphere of hospitality, gaiety and friendliness. Even her canary in its cage in the window was as cheerful in adversity as its owner, singing away as though it looked out over a sunlit countryside instead of the bricks and mortar of a foggy slum.

I fancy Louie was consumptive; there were terrible coughing-fits, when, her face changing tragically, she would fumble for the ever-present crutches and struggle out somehow to the back-kitchen so that we should not be the embarrassed witnesses of her paroxysm. I doubt if she had long to live, poor soul; the fresh air and good food that might have saved her were as beyond her reach as the moon. She had so little to be happy about, and yet the only lasting memory I have of her is one of smiling green eyes and the gorgeous red head thrown back on the long, white neck while she laughed at her own jokes, a tinkling, pretty, spontaneous laugh as though she had the soundest lungs and the straightest limbs in the land.

Usually, of course, we were at home for tea, especially in the winter, when we would hurry along the dry, ringing pavements in the frosty air, with the sun already setting red behind the railway station. The warmth of the nursery would be comforting and Nanny, poking the banked-up fire into a yellow blaze, would soon produce that most tempting of all meals when you are hungry—nursery tea. A lightly-boiled egg, perhaps, a plate of freshly-cut, crusty bread and butter which, after the first two slices you could spread with jam or a sprinkle of brown sugar; sponge fingers, rock-cakes (Mrs Packer's could have had no truer appellation), and a mug of milk with a dash of tea to make you feel 'grown-up'.

In the street outside the lamp-lighter came by, his long stick tipped with fire over his shoulder, leaving in his wake the shining lamps of Ullin Street and St Leonard's Road. The fog was closing down on the River, for ships were blowing hoarsely in a distant, confused chorus, and somewhere down by Custom House a railway-engine was whistling anxiously. It would be time for Nanny to draw the curtains, so that the leaping flames glowed warmly on the great pink and crimson cabbage-roses with which they were patterned; and the two of us would sit companionably in the quiet nursery, silent save for the loud tick of an old alarm-clock on the mantelpiece and the rustling of the fire behind its high wire guard.

This was the hour when, to my joy, Nanny might suggest a 'sing-song'. Once you could persuade her to begin, she would go on and on until the inexorable guillotine of bed-time cut short the entertainment; for an entertainment it most certainly was. Nanny, blessed with a good ear and a clear, true voice, had an extensive repertoire. The Boer War was still so comparatively recent that its songs lived in people's memories: songs such as 'Soldiers of the Queen' and 'Good-bye, Dolly, I must leave you', and a splendid ditty in which some luckless child received at its christening the names of every general and battle of the South African campaigns. Then there were the latest hits of the day, 'Yip-yi-yaddy' and 'She sells sea-shells by the seashore' which caused endless hilarity in the nursery.

Best of all, in my estimation, were the songs that made you feel sad. With what sentimental warmth Nanny and I together would sing 'Clementine' and 'Swanee River'—I could easily have wept over those poor, exiled darkies—and that prime favourite, 'Just a Song at Twilight'! From there it was but an easy transition to the hymns that Nanny, since she had been trained in a convent choir, knew and loved so well that she sang them with a simple sincerity: rousing hymns like 'The Church's One Foundation' and 'Stand up, stand up for Jesus'; rollicking mission hymns, unknown to the sedate pages of Ancient & Modern, for St Frideswide's, like St Michael's, was always launching missions upon the more unresponsive areas of its parish; and those we classified as 'Sunday evening hymns', such as 'Abide With Me', 'Lead, Kindly Light', and 'Nearer My God to Thee', which had not yet become irre-vocably linked in people's minds with the fate of the *Titanic:* hymns that soothed and comforted by their very familiarity, as though their constant repetition over the years and the generations bestowed its own virtue more potent than the revolutions of a prayer-wheel!

As an educationalist Nanny was superb, the equal, I should imagine, of any highly-trained young lady with a 'system'. For one thing, she was a mine of fascinating information, of those saws, sayings, and expedients that in later life one takes for granted. When your store of worldly knowledge is still quite small, there is all the charm of novelty, the wonder of newly-acquired wisdom, in being told that new shoes squeak because you haven't paid for them; that the north wind doth blow, then you will have snow; and that tea can be defined as 'the cup that cheers but not inebriates'. It was Nanny who introduced me to that mysterious Mr Manners, for whom one always left something on the plate. As millions of children must have done, I pictured this curious personage, thin, dark, and anxious, daily haunting the scullery for whatever he could pick up: considerably more real than that awful warning against over-politeness, the poor gentleman who died swallowing a hot potato because he was far too well-behaved to spit it out!

It was Nanny who taught me—in addition to the 'three R's'—to say my prayers, to hem, buttonhole and feather-stitch, to sew on buttons firmly—not 'with a hot needle and thread' as the shop-people did—and to set in a sleeve. It was Nanny who showed me how to make paste for my scrap-album out of flour and hot water, and how to grow mustard-and-cress on damp flannel in the nursery window-boxes. It was Nanny who covered my ill-used and tattered story-books neatly in brown paper and wrote on them their titles in her beautiful, clear and flowing hand which is as firm today at the age of eighty as it was fifty years ago. It was Nanny who nursed me through all the minor ailments, Nanny who allayed my panic fears when the nursery ceiling fell down in a cloud of plaster, and on another terrible occasion when the nursery

chimney caught fire with an angry roar; Nanny who, when
we encountered a herd of bullocks in a narrow, high-hedged
Devonshire lane, realised that I was wearing *red*, and with
the utmost presence of mind backed my go-cart into a gateway and threw a dark blanket over until the danger was past:
an experience that impressed indelibly upon my mind the
alarming possibilities of the countryside as opposed to those
in towns.

And it was Nanny who collected gradually, over a period
of months, the 'presentation plates' of Christmas Annuals,
coloured illustrations from magazines and catalogues, from
grocers' calendars and discarded nursery books, to make my
'picture-screen'. When she considered that she had enough
material, the virgin screen, already neatly covered with sheets
of stout brown paper, would be laid upon the nursery floor,
and Nanny, on her hands and knees, to the accompaniment
of unrestrained excitement, would perform the tremendous
task of 'laying-out' and then 'pasting-on', the odd corners
being filled with 'scraps'—little coloured drawings of flowers,
fruit, animals and fairies that one could buy for a few pence a
sheet at Mr Seager's.

The screen stood round my bed; and over the years of
childhood and adolescence I have studied it so often that I
need only shut my eyes to see again those bright, familiar
pictures: the elegant Edwardian ladies in motoring-hats and
waisted fur-coats; the fleet of big yachts racing off Cowes; a
nauseatingly skittish little girl in a very *décolletée* dress tying
her own sun-bonnet on to the head of a long-suffering spaniel;
a painting called 'Dignity and Impudence' which represented
with indifferent art an enormous bloodhound, chin on paws,
being annoyed by a Skye terrier; a Christmas scene, all red
sunset, white snow, and cottages with lamplit windows;
some of Kate Greenaway's illustrations to *John Gilpin*, rescued before the book disintegrated under heavy nursery
pressure; a bunch of daffodils, very lifelike, from a calendar,

with the date, 1907, across the top. How time was flying! I was already well into my fifth year! The screen, if I possessed it now, would evoke with perfect clarity the sentiments, the opulence, the faint condescension, and perhaps the first stirrings of that new century and age that were agitating already the heavy drapes of Victorian hypocrisy and Gladstonian *laisser faire*.

Nanny at that time was indisputably the pivot upon which my limited world revolved. Nanny was all-sufficing, constant, stable as a rock in a world of uncertainties. Even today she still inspires the same confidence, convinces me that she still knows what is best to do in any eventuality. She is, as ever, sensible, reassuring, eminently realistic, a mistress of understatement.

'Fancy,' she observes when one makes some perturbing pronouncement, and proceeds to debate the most practical solution to the problem. Nothing seems to ruffle or excite her. I have a feeling that, should I tell her: 'Nanny! Nanny! The end of the world has come!' she would reply 'Fancy!' in that flat, unemotional tone of hers, thus reducing the whole cataclysm to the manageable level of a nursery *contretemps*.

9. 'Matthew, Mark, Luke and John'

THE letter, a single sheet preserved by chance, headed simply 'The Clergy House' and dated 'Christmas Eve, 1908', is signed by the four assistant priests then attached to St Michael's. Each has appended his Bachelor of Arts degree —one Lond:, two Oxons:, and a Cantab:—a formality clearly dictated by a sense of the auspiciousness of the occasion, for the letter runs:

> *Dear Vicar,*
>   *Turkey, etc: to hand. Herewith the undersigned tender their sincerest gratitude from the bottom of their hearts for your kindness. Best wishes of even date to you and yours.*

The Clergy House, acquired by my father as the only solution to the problem of a suitable lodging for his staff, consisted of two ordinary, dingy 'terrace' houses next door to the church in Teviot Street. They had been knocked into one; and here, in a fraternal and probably untidy *mènage*— I have no idea of their domestic arrangements and only one of them was ever married—lived those four good men whose austere black skirts overawed me so unaccountably when they assembled at the Vicarage on Monday mornings: a piece of unnecessary stupidity, for they were no strangers to me, either in or out of church. Their signatures on a scrap of yellowing paper—the ink is still dark enough—are perfectly sufficient to recall their personalities to my mind, although I must admit to following the regrettable practice, common among the laity, of assessing them largely by their capabilities in taking the service.

Naturally, in my opinion nobody could equal my father, either as celebrant or preacher; and the curates came in for some fairly searching criticism by comparison. Fr Matthew could sing in tune and Fr Mark could not; Fr Luke preached well and Fr John did not; in fact, when Fr John was seen to be making his way towards the pulpit as we sang the concluding clauses of the Nicene Creed, a weight of resignation fell upon one's shoulders at the prospect of fifteen minutes or so of boredom during which it would be desirable to adopt some means of passing the time, such as counting the red and black bricks in a certain arch, or tracing the meanderings of a strip of metal in the wrought-iron screen.

Say what you will—and I have often in later years heard my father rebuke those who set too much store by sermons—the ability to preach with eloquence, still more to convey a message with conviction, is a valuable asset to a priest, just as the gift of oratory outweighs in usefulness more estimable qualities in a politician. Often the matter of these sermons was well above my head—unless they told stories, which, bearing in mind the simple mentality of the average Poplar congregation, they often did. But to a child the presentation of a dish is more important than its ingredients, and it was the manner of their preaching that I found by far the most intriguing.

There was the aforesaid Fr John, fresh-faced, early turning grey, gentle and humble, with the calm, serene gaze of a saint, his sincerity and earnest faith trembling for expression on his lips—yet unable to frame his thoughts with force or clarity and capable of but one monotonous gesture in the pulpit. Moreover, he suffered from a distressing inability to stop. On at least one occasion, when he had preached for nearly twice his allotted time (seventeen minutes being the maximum at morning service) and the hearts of the congregation were growing heavy with apprehension over the fate of their Sunday dinners, while still poor Fr John, becoming visibly perturbed, could find no way of bringing his circumlocutions to an end, my father, listening from the sanctuary, commanded one of his acolytes to strike a loud blow upon the sanctus bell. The single note ringing like a clarion through the silent church affected the unfortunate Fr John like the breaking of a spell. He started, blushed, looked wildly round, and pronouncing a hurried blessing, fled from the pulpit.

Even this miscalculation of time pales before the achievement of a visiting priest who had been invited to conduct the Good Friday Three Hours' Service on the Seven Words from the Cross, and by ten minutes past four had just settled down comfortably to the Fourth Word! My father, who had been preaching elsewhere, had already returned to the Vicarage and was wondering why my mother had not appeared for the usual Good Friday meal of tea and Hot Cross buns. Luckily, realisation of his phenomenal tardiness came suddenly to the visitor, who, abandoning all pretence of finishing his address conventionally, simply announced the last hymn and vanished.

Of our curate Fr Matthew, severe, ascetic, very dark and solemn, I had once overheard my father remarking that he was somewhat saturnine. I mistook this for satanic, which in view of his calling, seemed a curiously contradictory epithet; and Nanny, who as a devotee of St Frideswide's was unfamiliar with our clergy in their professional capacity, very properly refused to discuss their personal qualities. I remained unenlightened for years; in any case, Fr Matthew's sermons were so intellectual and of such lofty moral calibre that I doubt if I ever attempted to follow them. He was a man of high principles and strong convictions, who would make of them a scourge for his own back: a man who appeared in the eyes of a child to be remote and seldom happy.

For sheer dramatic interest you could always rely upon Fr Luke, a merry, vigorous person, friendly and kind to children, but metamorphosed in the pulpit, where apparently he donned a prophet's robe with the stole that he would place so deliberately around his neck before arranging his notes portentously upon the reading-desk and giving out his text with a deceptive quietness. Then, fixing the congregation with a steely eye, he would deliver himself of an opening sentence in tones of impressive gravity. He had a very loud voice, and when he wished, could thunder like a very Boanerges. The parishioners of St Michael's, I imagine, must have fancied him enormously. He was fond of employing a technique that can best be described as 'dangling them over the everlasting fires', and often in the midst of his fulminations I would feel uncomfortably certain that it was *my* sins of which he was giving such an eloquent description, *my* ultimate fate that he delineated with such horrifying lucidity. Glowering at his hearers while he worked up to a climax, his eyes seemed to grow larger and brighter, his face to become more lined and harrowed with the consciousness of sin; even his hair—he was rapidly getting bald—appeared to stiffen and start from its place with combined remorse, grief, and righteous indignation at the follies of mankind.

Out of church I liked him well enough, whenever we might run across each other in the study, the hall, or the garden—or the Tumty Room on the stupendous annual occasion of the Christmas Tree. But my favourite after all, was Fr Mark, he who, try as he might, could not sing in tune: a minor fault easily outweighed in my estimation by his endearing qualities of simplicity, cheerfulness and accessibility. Intellectually, I believe, he was the most brilliant of them all; as to that, I was totally indifferent; I merely knew instinctively that I could show him my own particular plot of garden and his interest in it would not be the usual grown-up's simulation, but reality. *He* did not smile at the ridiculous arrangement of my plants; nor at the treasures in my 'museum', a glass-fronted cabinet which housed a weird collection of such objects as odd relics of my parents' foreign holidays, dolls in national dress, and some scraps of Polynesian tappa-cloth acquired from a missionary exhibition.

Whether through kindness, exquisite politeness, or a natural comprehension of the child-mind, he paid me the compliment of giving serious consideration to my affairs. A child may understand well enough that its petty pre-occupations cannot genuinely be of much importance to a grown-up, but they are nevertheless of immense concern to the child itself, and such adult attention induces confidence.

Fr Mark had very bright blue eyes set in a brown face which curiously conveyed a certain suggestion of the Orient in its bone-structure; it was possible to perceive a faint similarity with the faces of the Chinamen in the West India Dock Road. When about the year 1910 he decided to go as a missionary to Korea, his destination seemed entirely fitting, although I do not know what called him in particular to that distant country beyond an imperious need to obey the summons of his Master.

He sailed from Tilbury in a brand-new ship called the *Morea*, on what I believe to have been her maiden voyage. My parents, who went to the Dock to see him off, thought it better not to take me with them, despite my entreaties to be allowed to go; it was to be another sixteen years before I first set eyes on the impressive black hull and funnels, the stone-coloured upperworks of a mail-ship belonging to the Peninsular & Oriental Steam Navigation Company—that partnership of colour and form unequalled at sea for its extraordinary implication of powerfulness, efficiency and distinction—with which in later life I was to become exceedingly familiar.

In the mission-field Fr Mark was set a task of extreme difficulty, travelling alone over vast tracts of uncivilised countryside while in the process of disentangling the fantastic complications of the Korean language. That he had to learn it at all posed me a riddle over which I puzzled long. What had happened to the gift of tongues bestowed upon the Apostles at Pentecost—those Apostles of whom Fr Mark and my father, and indeed all properly ordained Anglican clergymen, were the direct spiritual heirs through the Apostolic Succession? The Gospel for Whit Sunday says unequivocally that 'every man heard them speak in his own language', and that included Cretes and Arabians, and presumably Koreans as well, if some had happened to be there. Did this miraculous power die with the Apostles? Why could it not be transmitted together with the power to bind and to loose, to retain and to remit? It was one of those minor theological points upon which a child's intelligence seizes, while grown-ups take it comfortably for granted. I never summoned up sufficient courage to seek elucidation—and the problem remained unsolved.

One of Fr Mark's letters to my parents, written in May, 1911, from The Clergy House, Kanghon, expresses some of his doubts and difficulties: 'I am off to Paik Chun and complete isolation tomorrow. . . . There is a physical strain on workers here through continuous itinerating, but I venture to say—after the initial struggle with the vernacular —the tax on brain is very small. . . . If the work is to last there's got to be thinking done and planning with an eye

on the future. . . . Now you must all just buck us up and get
us strength and wisdom for the job in hand—it's not easy
going. . . .' Yet in the midst of this exacting new life he
could remember to send a doll dressed in a long white coat
and a high black Korean hat—'for the museum'.

Fr Mark was to die in Korea; his body is buried somewhere
in the city of Seoul, never to return from that strange,
remote, inhospitable 'Land of Morning Calm' for which,
nevertheless, he developed a kind of rueful affection. I
cannot recall who took his place: perhaps the round-faced,
swarthy little Ulsterman, or the tall, fair 'Honourable'
who used to take his Boy's Club annually to his home 'up
West' where his housekeeper would provide them with such
a feast that even they had to admit repletion. There were few
changes, most of the curates remaining with my father for
long periods. Under his determined captaincy they must
have composed a formidable combination of intellect,
energy and faith; yet I am unable to estimate the effect of
their cumulative assault upon the forces of ignorance, despair
and unbelief then flourishing in the parish, since I knew little
of their work beyond some chance occasion, such as when
Nanny and I attended suitable functions in the Parish Hall.

Usually these were unsophisticated entertainments provided by some of my parents' Lancaster Gate friends with
a taste and turn for amateur theatricals who did not object
to an afternoon's 'slumming' for the benefit of the Mothers'
Union. At one of these a hitch occurred in the programme,
and the luckless Fr John, who must have been in charge of the
proceedings, was sent before the curtain to bridge the gap.

'Now, mothers,' he began, desperately shy and blushing
more furiously than ever under the amused but sardonic
gaze of the audience. 'What about a song to fill in the time?
What is that one you know so well—"We all go the same
way home"?'

The mothers burst out laughing. Of course they knew

it well! It was the song they roared out when they stumbled and reeled away from the pubs at closing-time! They roared it out now with a will, the sedate khaki-coloured walls of the Parish Hall echoing strangely to the boisterous ditty; and Fr John, delighted with their ready compliance, walked happily to and fro before them, beating time quite superfluously with one hand while he joined decorously in the singing.

Like everyone connected with the church either officially or otherwise, all the curates turned their hands to any kind of job at that event of such enormous significance in parochial life in those days: the Annual Church Bazaar. Only in a few village communities, more isolated than most, can a Sale of Work still excite those feelings of pleasurable anticipation and innocent rivalry that our Church Bazaar aroused each year in the breasts of those who took part in it. The fevers of preparation passed practically unnoticed over my head, save for such indications of its approach at the Vicarage as extra activity by the working-party in the Tumty Room, and the arrival of various interesting objects for the White Elephant Stall; but it would not surprise me to learn that its successful organisation entailed nearly twelve months' work by the devoted few.

A White Elephant Stall, incidentally, must not be confused with mere Jumble, none of which is allowed at the Bazaar: you do not mix the two sorts of merchandise, for in a parish like St Michael's—indeed, in many others where the people are a good deal better off—the kind of person who comes to a Jumble Sale is not the kind of person you want to have at a proper Bazaar: they have little money to spend, and they are not above stuffing a few articles for which they have not paid into capacious oilskin bags—shoplifting was a widespread industry in Poplar. The Jumble Sales, in the natural order of things, had been held earlier in the year, for there is a certain protocol in the conduct of such affairs, a sequence of events laid down by custom. Money has first to be raised in small amounts so that you may raise more later in large amounts. The degree of energy implied is quite incalculable, and people will sigh over the work that must be done. It would be so much easier, one would think, just to subscribe a sum of money and be done with it; but let someone suggest the expedient and eyebrows will go up with disapproval. It would rule out all the bustle, the importance, the sense of being involved in something— in fact, the cultivation of a corporate feeling that is such an estimable by-product of these functions.

St Michael's Jumble Sales, of which I can but speak by hearsay, were formidable affairs. Only the toughest, shrewdest parish workers were chosen to act as saleswomen; Mr Morgan, the Verger, a retired sailor up to anybody's tricks, with a peaked cap, a stiff leg and a ginger moustache, was always present, keeping his gimletty blue eye upon the customers; and the police were usually invited to attend. The action, I believe, was short, sharp, and fought with the utmost tenacity on either side.

Great pains were taken to provide an interesting setting for the Bazaar itself. It was not to be passed off lightly as just *a* Bazaar, or even *the* Bazaar. You were bidden to spend an afternoon or evening 'In Picturesque Holland'—cardboard windmills, artificial tulips, and the stallholders dressed appropriately in Dutch caps, roomy petticoats, and clogs— or 'In Old Japan', when everybody wore kimonos and stuck paper chrysanthemums in their hair.

'Queer-looking lot of Japanese,' someone is reported to have said—probably a seafarer who knew the Far East— as he regarded the rotund blondes, the sandy, raw-boned Cho-Cho-Sans of Ullin Street. The men, with their usual self-consciousness, refused to dress up, which was felt to be a pity: Maggie's stately father alone would have looked magnificently in keeping as a Samurai.

I saw nothing incongruous in these affairs. It was always exciting to turn one's back on the foggy, smoky, damp November afternoon, mount the stone stairs to the large hall on the first floor, pay one's entrance pennies to Mr Morgan, who held the door, peaked cap, stiff leg, piercing blue eye and all, and be made free of the place, transformed by unaccustomed crowds, lights, decorations, and a rich mixture of Poplar smells diluted by the subtler odours of tea-urns, lavender-bags, and home-made sweets.

Usually I would be given five shillings to spend: a respectable sum of money then. First of all, it was necessary to make a comprehensive tour in order to see how to lay out one's capital to the best advantage. The stalls, on the whole, were far less interesting to a small girl than the sideshows. For the price of twopence you could inspect the 'Art Gallery', annual product of much ingenuity on the part of one of the curates and the Men's Bible Class. The exhibits were not hung on the walls, as one might expect, but were laid out on shelves. 'A Study in Oils,' said the label beside a tin of sardines; 'A Town in Ireland' was represented by a cork; 'Have I caused thee tears, my darling?' belonged to a large Spanish onion—in my view, the supreme example of wit in the whole collection.

'We go one better than Lloyd George: Two Bob for Twopence!' proclaimed the notice over a booth next door. Here you could try your hand at fishing for a glimmering florin placed innocently enough at the bottom of a basin of water. But the miraculous march of science in 1910 had preserved it from greedy fingers by passing a mild electric current through the water, and the struggle between rapacity and pain was often accompanied by shrieks.

It was obligatory to visit the fortune-telling lady, she who read our fates in the tea-cups when we went to call on her. A dressmaker by profession, she was devoted to the church and thought nothing of sitting up into the small hours to finish the stallholders' costumes in time for the Bazaar. She had a passion and a talent for telling fortunes; and with her extremely black eyes, hair like a raven's wing and smooth, sallow skin, she looked as though she might very well have inherited a strain of gipsy blood. She was vividly amusing, inexhaustibly energetic, and unquenchably cheerful. I have never met anyone her equal for sheer volubility: a useful asset in fortune-telling. The words rattled from her lips with the tireless precision and the pace of a machine-gun, while her fingers flickered over the cards and those sharp, ebony eyes darted between the table and her client's face.

Unfortunately, the austere Fr Matthew, presenting his usual uncompromising front to the hosts of Midian, had forbidden her under pain of his severe displeasure to foretell the future. This spoiled everything. Just as she was getting well into her stride, the cards obliging handsomely with long journeys, large sums of money and wealthy suitors, she would break off in genuine perturbation, exclaiming: 'Oh, my goodness! Father Matthew has made me promise not to do that!'

The whole afternoon would pass in a glorious, heated, bustling welter of spending and guessing competitions and sideshows—including an entertainment at which Maggie would recite the poems of Mr Geo. R. Sims with what seemed to me to be outstanding elocutionary skill—ending up with an enormous sixpenny tea—I fancy the Vicar's younger daughter got rather more than her fair share of cakes—and at last, and all too soon, an inexorable yet patient Nanny repeating: 'Now come along, it's past your bedtime!'

Only once did I dread the occasion of the Church Bazaar instead of looking forward to it. The distinguished visitor from the West End who was to open it—by virtue of a reputation for good works and a purse stuffed with gold sovereigns—fell ill at the very last moment, and it seemed that the customary opening ceremony would have to be abandoned. But my father, possessor of those truly British qualities, a genius for improvisation and an unwillingness to submit to obstacles, suddenly thought of a solution. I was sent for to go to the study at some extraordinary hour of the day.

'How would *you* like to open the Bazaar?'

I did not like it at all. I was then extremely shy, and the prospect of standing up all by oneself in that great space, of hearing the sound of one's own voice when nobody else was speaking, struck me as something quite impossible for me to achieve. But I would have done anything to please my father, and naturally I agreed.

'You needn't make a speech. Stand up over there, very straight, and say as loud as you can: "I declare this Bazaar open!"'

'I—declare—this—Bazaaropen!'

'Not "Bazaaropen. Bazaar—open"'

We had endless trouble with that simple sentence before I was able to apply to the vowel 'o' what I believe is known to teachers of singing as the 'glottal plosive'. I was taken to the hall itself and made to repeat that frightful announcement from the actual spot on the platform whence I should be required to make it on the day itself—I imagine all this to have taken place some twenty-four hours beforehand. Somebody—one of the curates, I am almost certain—lurking in the shadows at the back of the hall, infinitely far away, called out that he could just hear me—only just. But it would have to do. All next day the hours rolled relentlessly towards the fatal moment while I endured every known agony of stage-fright.

'Got butterflies in your tummy?' inquired my father; and endeavoured to hearten me with an account of his rowing days when he had experienced exactly the same symptoms while paddling to the stakeboat and passing down the sweaters.

I felt as though borne helplessly towards a whirlpool, destined to enter its vortex precisely at 2.30 that very afternoon. As in a dream I was dressed by Nanny in my Sunday hat and coat: an occurrence sufficiently upsetting of itself upon a weekday. Even she had no satisfactory comfort to offer me, not even that anodyne of desperation with which in later life I have so often consoled myself before some petrifying ordeal: 'At least they can't *eat* you!' None the less, on occasion, it is possible to wonder if there are not several worse fates than being eaten.

My father, smiling broadly, exuding confidence and encouragement, led me by the hand to the Parish Hall, along the green-painted wooden fence of the Vicarage garden—it had never seemed so long—past the west end of St Michael's—oh, if only I had been going to church!—and up the stairway to the place of sacrifice itself. He led me on to the platform; and I saw for the first time a sea of faces, curious, expectant, kindly. My father began to explain about the lady from the West End who had been taken ill.

'Rather than disappoint you we have gone to tremendous trouble and expense to provide a substitute. And we have found someone, after all, right on our own doorstep, someone who is well known to you all, someone who has the interests of St Michael's as much at heart as you have—someone, I think, who will surprise you all—my daughter!'

His hand on my shoulder pressed me firmly forward; and then, whether from the unexpectedness of my appearance or amusement at my agitated face I shall never know, but people in the hall began to laugh! It was horribly disconcerting; my knees were shaking already and my mouth was as dry as a sandpit—sensations to which at the age of seven or eight you are not accustomed. Someone called 'shush!' and instantly an appalling silence fell, in which I heard my father commanding softly: 'Go on!'

I said: 'I declare—this—Bazaaropen!'

I could have cried with mortification. I had done it wrong after all! I turned to rush from the platform but someone stopped me. There was a bouquet of flowers (doubtless ordered for the original opener) to be presented to me by another girl—could it have been Maggie?—who bobbed before me as though I had been royalty. I began to feel better; and when my mother, and Nanny, and Mrs Saunders and Mr Morgan and many more had all assured me admiringly that I had done it very well, I began to preen myself. For the first time I had tasted the sweets of public applause as a just reward for exerting oneself to perform a distasteful action!

The cassocked figures of the curates who should have loomed so largely in this chapter seem to have withdrawn themselves into the background—where, for all I can tell, they would much prefer to be. My memories of them, after all, are the merest faded scraps of material in an old patchwork of which so much is bright; and one of the clearest —summoned up by that letter written on Christmas Eve some fifty years ago—has nothing whatever to do with their professional activities.

Do children still long with every fibre of their beings for Christmas?—still shiver with anticipatory bliss at its approach? —abandon themselves gloriously to the extravagant ecstasies of its arrival?

For us the real excitement began on Christmas Eve, after tea, when we had our Christmas Tree in the Tumty Room. Dressed in my best frock, I would wait in a delicious agony of suspense in the nursery until Nanny came to tell me that I could go downstairs. That moment when I descended the three steps into the Tumty Room seemed to me the most entrancing instant of the festival: perhaps of the whole year. The Tumty Room appeared to have become a darkened, magic cave in which the central object was the illuminated pyramid of the tree itself, glowing with colour, heavy with

166

fascinating parcels, and flanked by a large and jolly Father Christmas. He had really come after all! He was a little frightening with his scarlet hood pulled well forward over his eyes and his bushy white beard hiding the rest of his face: sufficiently forbidding to preclude a close inspection, however much you longed to know exactly what he looked like.

My sister seemed to be on terms of comparative intimacy with him. Dressed as a fairy in a white skirt with a star in her hair and a silver wand, she skipped about the room handing round the presents. I thought her wonderful: a privileged intermediary between ourselves and the super-natural world inhabited by Father Christmas. When I could tear my eyes away from this gorgeous spectacle, I saw that my mother, smiling happily, had put on her 'Liberty' tea-gown specially for this great event; Elizabeth and Mrs Packer, a little shy at first but relaxing in the universal warmth, were sitting in the background; and the curates, too, were there. Doubtless, they wore on this occasion ordinary worldly suits of those sub-fusc materials common to clergymen in lay clothing; but my memory invariably depicts them dressed in those cassocks, a little shiny with wear and smelling slightly of incense, ceintured or belted, sometimes with a shoulder-cape; and their birettas.

Whatever they wore, they were no longer capable of inspiring the least degree of awe on that miraculous night when even Mrs Packer assumed a kindly aspect. They made jokes and sat on the floor and helped to undo parcels and admired everybody's presents—our toys, books, and dolls, the lengths of durable material or warm gloves and scarves for the servants—as well as whatever it was they themselves had been given. Like most children, I was far too deeply engrossed in what I myself had managed to acquire even to care from whom I had received it—it was the present and not the giver that mattered!

The only disappointing feature of this enchanted hour was the absence of my father, who was always too busy to come. This never occurred to me as odd; nor that, on one occasion when he did happen to be present, one of the curates was unable to be there, and Father Christmas that year seemed to be very much smaller and thinner and less gruff than usual.

Very gradually, as time went on and each Christmas Tree came round again, a nasty little viperish doubt glided into my mind that Father Christmas was not really a person from the fairy world but a mortal being dressed up to represent him. I repelled this horrible idea because I did not want to believe it; I dreaded the moment when I might *have* to believe it; and eventually, of course, in the middle of some furious argument about something entirely different, my sister, to prove my babyishness and gain her point, exclaimed: 'And don't you know, you little fathead, that Father Christmas is only *Daddy?*'

And that, I suppose, is the closing of the first little gate of the many by which one is excluded, inexorably, piecemeal, from the garden of childhood where, at the beginning, one wanders at will.

However, happily enough throughout those early years, I saw Father Christmas depart through the door leading to the back premises on his way to visit another lucky household; and was agreeably surprised at the arrival of my father shortly afterwards, smoothing down his hair, and anxious to be shown all our splendid new toys. And if Christmas Eve was over for another year, there was still the morrow: morning church with Christmas hymns; Christmas dinner with crackers; and afterwards, surfeited with food and excitement, one knelt up at the nursery window to watch for Grandpapa's car.

You could tell it at once from the ordinary traffic of St Leonard's Road by the two great yellow headlights, like the eyes of a huge cat, as it purred cautiously down the narrow street in the fog and murk of the late December afternoon. A huge, hearse-like Daimler with soft grey upholstery and driven by a tremendously efficient chauffeur in shining black gaiters and a peaked cap, it had come to fetch the whole family, and Nanny too, to stay at Grandpapa's big house in Kent.

10. Rural Pursuits

THE squalid and utilitarian environs of the Blackwall Tunnel
—through which the Daimler, gliding almost soundlessly,
transported us to the Kentish shore—did not comprise my
whole world; neither was it bounded entirely by that somewhat turbid trio of waterways, the Limehouse Cut, Bow
Creek, and the London River.

Both sets of grandparents and an occasional aunt would
invite me, accompanied, of course, by Nanny, for visits, either
when my parents went abroad, or on the pretext that I needed
country air. But I preferred not to be parted for long from my
father and mother, and it was to the huge family gathering
at Christmas-time that I looked forward with the warmest
pleasure.

Surrounded by lawns, a belt of shrubberies and miles of
open common-land, my paternal grandfather's house, although
only fourteen miles from Charing Cross, represented in my
eyes the extreme of rural isolation. However sleepy I might
be at bedtime, I found it difficult to accustom myself to the
utter silence of the country night. No traffic clattered past

THE SHABBY PARADISE

under the windows, nobody shouted or yelled across the street, no convivial songs disturbed the peace, no ships or tugs blew their sirens on a distant river. My only solace was the far-off whistle of a train from the nearest station a good three miles away. An owl would hoot eerily in the encircling trees; at times it seemed to be drifting past the very window, and my Cockney heart would pound with fear, so that I was obliged to scream for Nanny, enjoying her supper in some distant region of that immense house.

There was a wing, much older than the rest, in which we grandchildren were never put to sleep. A bedroom—seldom used—was haunted in the most original manner. No ghost was ever seen or heard, but from outside the house the room appeared to be brilliantly lit up and the door resisted all attempts to open it. When this curious manifestation was first observed, my grandmother concluded that a burglar was inside. She promptly ordered the door to be broken down; but the room was found to be in darkness, the windows closed, nothing disturbed or taken. No solution was ever discovered; still, at rare intervals, the light shone from the unoccupied room, the door refused to open; then, all at once, the evocation, whatever it may have been, passed away; the latch could be turned once more, revealing nothing but darkness, emptiness and silence.

The house had once belonged to a Prime Minister of England, and in my grandfather's day it was at least as prosperous, if somewhat less distinguished. After his death, like a ship that has run off her class and suffers a decline in fortune in consequence, it became a school. Now, in what might be termed the final stage of deterioration when no alternative offers but the breaker's yard, it shelters officials of one of the more Communist-ridden trade unions. In actual fact, the comparison no longer holds; for the carriage of emigrants and even coolies—final chapter in many a ship's career—is at least an honourable and useful activity. But per-

172

haps those heads, stuffed with empty ideologies and burdened
with sterile preoccupations, do not rest so easily o' nights
beneath that handsome roof; that uneasy evocation, to whatever century it may have belonged, would not, I fancy, approve
of Communism.

At Christmas-time the house would seem bewilderingly
full of people, of aunts and uncles, cousins, servants and dogs,
horses and grooms, all to be remembered and recognised
anew; for to the very young, as to the very old, remembering
is sometimes difficult. My grandfather himself, slight, quiet,
tired-looking, with mutton-chop whiskers and an air of something only to be described as a power of latent authority
which even a small child could understand, had little to do
with us. I was very much in awe of him. Except on Sundays
and holidays, I saw him always dressed in formal city clothes,
a black coat and a silk hat, which he would smooth carefully
with his handkerchief as he said good-bye to Granny in the
hall after breakfast. I had no clear idea of what he was, or
what he did, save that he went off every morning in the
Daimler to London and returned shortly before my bedtime,
when we were allowed downstairs to watch him having tea
in Granny's vast drawing-room, full of Sèvres and Rockingham
and Crown Derby, of brass standard lamps with pleated silk
shades, gilt-framed water-colours, fluffy white rugs, and
enormous, elaborately-upholstered sofas.

The house, indeed, conveyed a sense of security and wealth
which I could tell was in great contrast to the adequate but
shabby comforts of St Michael's Vicarage. There were deep
soft carpets covering every inch of floor, even in the landings
and passages. There were bronze statues and massive clocks,
huge oil-paintings in heavy frames, solid pieces of Victorian
mahogany furniture, a billiard-room where we played at Red
Indians under the table when the grown-ups did not wish to
play upon it. Upstairs there were bedrooms far larger than
any rooms I had ever seen. There were four bathrooms, all

installed by my grandfather and considered in those days to be carrying the modern craze for plumbing to the point of lunacy. There were labyrinthine kitchens, larders, store-rooms and pantries opening off a long stone passage walled in by creeper-covered trellis-work and leading eventually to the stables. Our nursery quarters, sensibly secluded above the kitchen, were reached by an interminable corridor—corresponding to the stone passage—not very well lit, down which I advanced at night with some trepidation. It was lined for its whole length with bookshelves, upon which stood a variety of stuffed birds under glass covers: and half-way along it was a large and malignant owl, whose glaring yellow eye seemed to move as you passed. For years I nursed an uneasy suspicion that it was identical with the owl that hooted so frighteningly of nights outside my window.

Even this ample accommodation was strained at Christmas-time, when the entire family gathered under one roof. My grandparents had eight children, seven of whom were then married, five of them with families of their own. Thus five sets of children invaded the house, and more formidable still, five nannies who had to be persuaded to co-operate, not only with each other, but with the household. There were disagree-ments and scenes; each nanny, not unnaturally, considered her own charges the most important and her own methods of management the only satisfactory ones. My grandmother, stout, affable and energetic, a woman of great character and mercifully of great humour as well, ruled the whole houseful with easy authority. There was never any doubt as to who was mistress of that establishment; and if she wished to dele-gate her powers, she did so with perfect confidence to the head parlourmaid, Green, a terrifying person who fulfilled all the requirements of a sort of feminine R.S.M. in black and white. Tall and spare, with a chest flat as a board beneath the starched bib of her apron, her grey hair neat as a wig under a small mob-cap from which two streamers floated, she never seemed to relax and seldom smiled. She had, apparently, no existence beyond the performance of her duties, handing dishes with impeccable correctitude in her deep, stiffened cuffs, standing rigidly as any guardsman behind my grandmother's chair at meals, fetching her handbag, her clean handkerchief, her bottle of pills: the epitome of the trained, devoted servant of those days.

It was all very confusing to a child unused to so much company. Fires blazed in every room, at dusk lights streamed from every door and window. On Christmas Night, when we kept awake with difficulty in order to be dressed in our party-frocks and go down to the dining-room for dessert, the sight of the great mahogany table loaded with silver and glass, piled with fruit and nuts and delicacies of which I did not even know the names, and surrounded by grown-ups in evening-dress, was altogether too much for me. Granny would encircle each one of us in turn with an affectionate arm while she pressed on us a *marron glacé*, some grapes, a crystallised pear, a Carlsbad plum; but overcome with shyness, I would be thankful to run and hide my face in my father's ample black silk waistcoat.

Not that people were unkind. My cousins were friendly enough, but disconcertingly self-confident. They teased me mercilessly (which I needed badly), and with the natural snobbery of children, not in the least because I lived in the slums, but because I could not ride. Never having been in Poplar, they were maddeningly oblivious to the impossibility of keeping ponies there, even if my father had been able to afford it. The boy-cousins found me shy, timid, and bad at all games; the girl-cousins thought me uninteresting because I did not care for dolls or clothes.

The grown-ups talked above my head of politics: I knew by now that Liberals and Radicals were shady, incompetent and even wicked, and would eventually ruin the country unless the Conservatives soon got back in power; there were

endless discussions about Ulster, Home Rule, Mr Redmond
and Sir Edward Carson; there were arguments about religion
—my father being 'high church' and nearly all the rest of the
family extremely 'low'; and there were always long, incomprehensible conversations about ships and things to do with
ships.

It was not until after my grandfather's death just before
the First World War, at the comparatively early age of sixty,
that I discovered his eminence in the business world as a
metallurgist and engineer of unusual ability; he was not, as
I had always imagined, because he went to work so early and
came back so late, a kind of superior clerk, perched all day on
a counting-house stool, but chairman of a flourishing engineer-
ing firm. Meanwhile, I had absorbed unconsciously the names
of ships and shipping companies and even firms of ship-
builders, so that when I had more to do with them in later
life, many of them were familiar; they flowed back into my
mind, easily and as if by custom, from some long-shut pocket
of the memory. Of course, I knew well enough exactly what
a big ship looked like, from my intimacy with the Docks; and
flaunted this knowledge as a counter to my cousins' undoubted
superiority over horses.

Those stables, tacked on to the house beyond the kitchen
wing, accommodated a horse or a pony for everyone, it
seemed. My father hunted Grey Ghost, an enormous beast
with a hard mouth and an uncertain temper; to me he appeared
the height of a house. My cousins, uncles and aunts, all knew
how to ride and enjoyed following hounds. I neither rode nor
knew anything about horses; I was also guiltily aware that I
was frightened of them. To me there was nothing in the least
pleasurable about strolling over to the stables after breakfast
and feeding them with lumps of sugar. Horses, like dogs,
know only too well who fears them. Bidden to reach up and
stroke the animal's muzzle—not at all 'velvety', as novelists
describe it, but hard and hairy—I would do so, and the beast

176

would at once toss its head and roll its eyes in an alarming manner as though I had offended it mortally. Even more terrifying was the experience of proffering sugar on one's palm.

'He won't hurt you, you juggins! He'll take it as gently as a kitten!' my father, or aunt or uncle would assure me. But I thought there was nothing in the least gentle about the large, champing teeth and hard wet lips that snatched the lumps from my trembling hand.

It was no use; I was hopeless with horses. That must be put right, my grandfather said mildly; only somehow his mildness was more imperative than another's severity. He was genuinely anxious for me to savour the delights of horsemanship; for in those days the majority of people rode because they liked it, and not because the ability to do so bestowed a fancied *cachet* of gentility. Such things as Pony Clubs were unheard of; and no one expected you to feed, water, rub down or saddle your own mount. If you kept horses, automatically you employed grooms to look after them, instead of entrusting them to the uncertain ministrations of enthusiastic amateurs.

Moreover, any animal that happened to be available was considered good enough for an apprentice-hand. In my own case, a fat, docile, and elderly white pony who drew the mowing-machine at a funereal pace about the lawns in summer and ate his head off in winter, was nominated to bear me to meets of the Old Surrey and Burstow. Jacket and breeches of brown corduroy velvet were made for me by my father's tailor; a small round beaver cap and brown buttoned gaiters completed my riding-rig. I was accoutred with everything save skill—and courage. On the broad back of Paddy I rode round and round the paddock under my father's eye; and eventually, a groom at my bridle, I went to my first meet.

I felt cold and numb with fright and hated every minute of it. Other small girls, handling their mounts expertly without the aid of grooms, passed to and fro jauntily while I sat, miserably inactive, on Paddy's table-like carcase. When large, tall horses came uncomfortably close, blowing noisily down their nostrils, I flinched uncontrollably. When the field moved off I was taken by surprise, nearly fell and had to be pushed back into the saddle by the groom, who did not seem to be in the best of tempers, for he tugged quite viciously at Paddy's leading-rein. When hounds found, he had to break into a run and Paddy into a trot; I was unable to synchronise my rise and fall correctly and Paddy, annoyed at my clumsy bumping, dropped to a walk. The groom, muttering something under his breath, started to haul us through a copse. It contained a stream, at which Paddy first baulked, then decided to jump it after all, and this time I fell off properly. The groom took me home and I was in disgrace. Only Nanny, as usual, was my never-failing comforter; it didn't matter, she said, if you couldn't ride well; there were lots of other more important things in life.

One sharp, frosty morning, hacking gloomily across the common beside my father on Grey Ghost, we met a motor car. From its brass radiator clouds of steam were pouring, and it made a fearful noise. The sedate Paddy shied, hauling on his leading-rein. Grey Ghost, equally startled, suddenly bit Paddy violently on the muzzle. The outraged Paddy reared, and I found myself, bawling with fright, somewhere underneath his belly. I was taken home, shattered, and everybody decided unanimously that it was sheer waste of time trying to teach me to ride.

That close relationship between horse and rider, said to be so delightful, ceased abruptly in the case of Paddy and myself. In summer he resumed his task of pulling the lawn-mower, and not even a flicker of recognition crossed his placid old face when I came to speak to him. I was an episode in his life, brief but distressing, that he preferred not to remember.

As for myself, I retired with happiness from the hunting-field. The feeling of disgrace, of inadequacy, was as nothing to the sensation of relief. Let my cousins ride well, let them enjoy being in at the kill and coming home with their faces bloodied; let them be superlatively good at cricket and croquet and excel at clock-golf! *They* had never in their lives stood on the deck of a sailing-ship—nor for that matter a steamer, except perhaps a cross-Channel packet; they had never set eyes on a real, pig-tailed Chinaman, let alone one who smoked opium. Moreover, the girls admitted that they would be frightened out of their wits if they were to meet a drunk man. I withdrew defensively behind a secret façade of superiority, nourished by a deep inner conviction that *my* future lay on the water!

Occasionally, when my parents managed to take a short foreign holiday, Nanny and I would be sent by ourselves to stay with Granny. The great house was seldom empty; mysterious visitors connected with Grandpapa's business came and went, although we had little contact with them. They were mostly foreigners—Egyptians or South Americans— but they seemed quite dull by comparison with the denizens of Poplar. To be a solitary guest was something of an ordeal. Having washed my hands very carefully and had my hair-ribbons retied by Nanny, I would be sent downstairs at lunch-time to find Granny.

'Luncheon is served,' Green would say with all the solemnity of an archbishop pronouncing a doxology, and we two, seated at one end of the enormous mahogany table, would be waited on with all the ritual of an important function through the sequence of soup (special thin toast for Granny), fish, meat, and such sweet confections as Mrs Packer never dreamed of. I was unaccustomed to helping myself, and did so but clumsily from the silver entrée dish proffered by Green. Her face would remain utterly expressionless, even when I dropped gravy on the table, or meringue on the carpet, or upset the salt-cellar or knocked over my tumbler of water. I would go hot with embarrassment, and wonder if Green had a very poor opinion of my table manners.

The Daimler being in London with Grandpapa, the victoria would take us into the nearest town for an afternoon's shopping if the day were fine. Green saw us off at the front-door, tucking the carriage-rug of smooth brown fur around our legs, handing Granny her purse and a little basket, and listening intently to some last instruction.

'And we shall be back to tea, Green.'

'Very good, ma'am.'

Then we were spanking off down the long drive between the high hedge of rhododendron on the one hand and the paddock on the other. It was not nearly so exciting as riding in the Daimler, but it was a very pleasant, rolling sort of motion, smooth and quiet; the low rumbling of the wheels on the dusty roads, the creaking of harness and the unhurried clip-clop of hooves made an agreeable accompaniment to our steady progress along the neat, green, Kentish lanes.

There was also a brougham in which, on occasion, Granny and I drove all the way up to London to shop at Messrs Shoolbred's in the Tottenham Court Road, where Granny, a short stout figure—but none the less majestic—in a bonnet, a black sealskin jacket and a magnificent sable stole, would confer with a posse of deferential gentlemen as we moved with deliberation through groves of substantial, highly-polished Edwardian furniture. A dull emporium to a child; more to my taste was Marshall & Snelgrove, Gorringe's or Dickins & Jones, where at least there were bright ribbons, materials, feathers and artificial flowers. The final call was invariably at the Civil Service Stores, for Granny was a life-long supporter of that excellent if less fashionable establish-ment. But Hyerson, the coachman, did not care for these excursions; the new motor-buses were increasing in numbers —getting too much of a good thing altogether. It was all very well for the horse-buses, grumbled Hyerson; they were used to all this traffic, but our horses were a different matter. In later years we used the Daimler; I never remember going to town by train.

A romantic circumstance invested Granny's girlhood with significance: she had known Garibaldi at a time when that picturesque adventurer had withdrawn from the scene of his tempestuous exploits to live in London. The exotic flavour of that expert guerilla in his scarlet cowboy shirt and wide-brimmed hat accorded ill with one's notions of Granny as a girl. Indeed, why that conventionally brought-up daughter of a prosperous and established civil engineer should have moved in such flamboyant and even revolutionary circles is a mystery; perhaps Great-uncle Reginald, the sailor brother, had met with Garibaldi in his seafaring days. He was connected in my mind with nothing more glamorous than a kind of biscuit and a vague representation of a wild-eyed person waving a flag upon a pinnacle of rock; and many times since then have I wished that Granny had lived longer, that I had known her better and learned from her own lips some truths about that highly-coloured hero.

Every Boxing Day the whole family would observe with enthusiasm the long-established ritual of attending the panto-mime at Drury Lane. The provider of this magnificent treat was my father's eldest sister—and *my* favourite aunt; and so large was the total sum of nieces and nephews, parents and nannies, that she was obliged to book a whole row of stalls right across the theatre.

I have no recollection of my first pantomime, for my father intended us to appreciate the theatre, of which he was extremely fond, and introduced us at a very early age to the delights of the London stage. In Edwardian days there was still a faint hesitation in accepting as absolutely normal a parson's interest in the theatre. Older people exclaimed: 'Broad-minded!' with a flick of the eyebrows and in that tone which children know very well implies some form of criticism only comprehensible to the adult world. This kind of broad-mindedness seemed to ally itself most naturally with the High Church party, for the old-fashioned Evangelical still held the theatre and all its works in abhorrence as direct inspirations of the devil.

My maternal grandfather was an example, pure and unde-filed, of this honourable if outmoded school. My mother, indeed, had never been to a theatre until she was taken to one after her marriage by my father, so utterly different had been her upbringing to his. This complete dissimilarity in their homes was easily discernible to us children. The large, bountiful house in Kent, always going at full pressure, always conveying, even to the young, an atmosphere of events, of affairs, of material well-being, ranked not unnaturally as the favourite in our affections, even if we found it a little alarming. By contrast, my mother's old home, scarcely further from London in the opposite direction, achieved an air of unworldly isolation that might have belonged to Jane Austen's Chawton in the depths of Hampshire. The cab-drive from the station through unpeopled country lanes, the quiet vicarage dreaming away the last decades of its existence—it has long been pulled down to make way for a housing-estate—in a garden of rose-bushes, lawns, and monkey-puzzle trees, perfectly prepared the visitor for the tranquil life led by my grandparents: kind but undemonstrative, comfortable without ostentation, cheerful without levity.

My grandfather was a scholar, a dreamer, a hermit, enclosed perpetually within the physical walls of his study and the spiritual ramparts of his immense reserve. My grand-mother, small, gentle, sweet, reminiscent of a sober-plumaged and industrious bird, went quietly about her parish works, or sat in the deep bay-window of her drawing-room embroider-ing the fabulously difficult designs for which she faded her silks to the required shades by leaving them in the summer sun. The whole house could have been lifted bodily into a museum as a perfect period piece of nineteenth-century clerical domesticity—a country parsonage of Victorian times: the oil-lamps, the hip-baths before a blazing bedroom-fire, with brown cakes of Windsor soap in a white china soap-dish; the flowered chintzes, the bowls of potpourri, the eighteenth-century family portraits in the drawing-room; the wood-panelling covered with cracked brown paint, the book-lined study smelling of cigars, which were my grandfather's one indulgence; the plain, but exquisitely-cooked meals of good, solid food, the sparingly-drunk Rhine wine in tall, slender bottles of dark-green glass.

Ungratefully, we children never looked forward with much enthusiasm to our visits to this abode of piety and peace. It seemed to us a little dull, and our grandfather's services extremely dreary by comparison with those at St Michael's. Grandpapa wore a long surplice like a nightgown; there was little singing; the congregation appeared to be most irreverent in their behaviour; and, being a stranger to Mattins, I could not find my way about the Prayer Book.

Grandpapa had the most exquisite manners, listening with as much grave courtesy to the trifling utterances of a grand-child as he would have done to the remarks of royalty; but his austere composure I found forbidding; and every morning, sharp at eight o'clock, there was the ordeal of Family Prayers, even then regarded as old-fashioned. On the stroke of the hour we assembled in the dining-room, the servants filing in after us in their crackling print-dresses. Although far from irreligious, I would be smitten with a strong desire to giggle as, rising from our chairs, we turned and knelt before them, burying our faces in their seats. How funny we should look if anyone came in just then! And how strange that, fifteen minutes later, we should find ourselves sitting calmly upon those very chairs, into the seats of which we had just been praying, to eat our breakfasts!

Family Prayers began the day also at the house of the

beloved aunt—the benefactress of the pantomime—who had married a clergyman, an Oxford friend of my father's: the family bristled on either side with ecclesiastics. But here the whole atmosphere was infinitely mellowed; that square, capacious, comfortable Queen Anne rectory resembled in character more nearly the great house in Kent, but on a smaller and less formal scale. The food was equally delicious —but there was no formidable Green to serve it. There were stables—but they sheltered nothing more terrifying than the fat chestnut pony that drew the trap in which my uncle met us at the station.

Separated from Poplar by a few short miles of the county of Middlesex, one passed in that brief transit to another world; it seemed impossible that trouble, insecurity, grief or illness could ever disturb those placid acres where my uncle and aunt spent their good and busy lives. Winter and summer alike, the place exuded the warmth of welcome, wrapped you in a kind of feather-bed of comfort. My aunt, plump, generous, affectionate and merry, bustled serenely but untiringly through the day. Early in the morning I would hear her in the stable-yard, calling to her hens like any farmer's wife; last thing at night, muffled in a heavy coat, a cap of astrakhan set securely on her thick brown hair, she would take the big labrador, Nigger, for his final walk about the lanes, however dark and moonless it might be. I thought her very brave; not for ten golden sovereigns would my craven Cockney soul have allowed me to venture down the drive! In between these two immovable activities she managed, firmly and beautifully, her household, the gardener, the church-workers, and the parish; entertained the neighbourhood at that hospitable and overflowing table; succoured the sick and impoverished; decorated the tiny Saxon church that she adored, and in which, to my joy, the Sunday morning service was entirely familiar; saw that my uncle was well wrapped up when he went out visiting or to choir practice; and in spare moments embroidered vestments, or worked at rugs and kneelers destined impartially, so far as I could tell, for church or rectory. In simple truth, she was a happy woman; and she repaid that happiness with compound interest to all with whom she came in contact.

In winter Nanny and I walked about the frosty lanes, returning with tremendous country appetites at lunch-time: a meal heralded by the most appetising smells that drifted up the back staircase—smells of baking pies, roasting game and chickens, boiling hams. In the afternoon there might be a children's party with games, fireworks and an incomparable tea; or my aunt might take me driving in the pony-trap, getting home in the nick of time to the enfolding warmth of the house as the wintry sun, huge and red, set, not behind chimneys, but through the bare boughs of surrounding cherry orchards.

But my memories of the place are mainly those of summer; perhaps, because I was always happy there, it seems to bask in the golden light of perpetual sunshine. The french windows beneath the trusses of wistaria in flower stand for ever open, admitting the drone of bees and the hum of a mowing-machine cutting the croquet-lawn; the standard roses along the winding path leading to the little, ancient church are always in bloom, scenting the warm air; there is deep shade beneath the enormous old yew hedge, thick and high as a battlement, through which an ample archway has been cut, and beneath the spreading copper-beech on the upper lawn, where a tea-party is in progress, with strawberries from the rectory garden and cream from the cows grazing in the water-meadows that slope gently to the looping Coln. There are home-made ices, too, and home-made lemonade for thirsty children to drink after a long, hot afternoon playing in the shallows of the river.

A child's Paradise, indeed, well-loved and familiar; but not so well-loved and not so familiar as the stale pavements of Poplar, the airless streets smelling of smoke and dirt and horse manure; the brassy sky obscured by fumes; our wilting garden; the dusty plane-trees and drooping privet; the grimy Vicarage which I did not seem to notice had grown a little shabbier, more threadbare and more in need of paint than ever.

I was always happy to come home.

11. Urban Diversions

WHEN the bare-footed children, regardless of their rags, ran behind the watering-carts for coolness, and the older folk, sitting on a rickety chair or an old box at the doorways of their oven-like homes, gasped for a breath of air, my mother would order a horse-drawn cab in which Nanny and I, accompanied by a carefully-packed tea-basket, would set off to visit Greenwich, across the River.

It was a little disappointing, of course, that people did not turn round to look after us as they would have done had we been in the Daimler: an attention very gratifying to my self-conceit until I discovered that they merely imagined the Daimler to contain the Bishop of London. But the passage through the Blackwall Tunnel alone made this expedition something of an adventure. The noise of the trotting horse echoed back loudly from the roof, and alarming streams of water poured down the white-tiled walls. I pictured the Thames, sparkling and choppy in the sunlight far above our heads, suddenly breaking through into the Tunnel, and was glad when we emerged on the other side.

The Greenwich shore attained, Nanny would tartly urge
the reluctant horse and cabby as far up Observatory Hill as
they could be made to go; and there we would have our
picnic-tea, almost in the shadow of the Observatory itself,
where I presumed the Astronomer Royal, surrounded by
telescopes, to be sleeping peacefully all day in preparation
for staring at the stars all night.

After the heat and noise of the East India Dock Road the
great slope of greensward, dotted in early summer with the
brilliant pink and white of blossoming may-trees, might have
been in the depths of the country. At our feet the classical
perfection of Greenwich College lay golden in the afternoon
sunlight. Beyond, like a painted backcloth, the panorama of
East London rose to the bright sky, the drab stipple of
innumerable roof-tops broken sharply by the soaring white
shafts of Nicholas Hawksmoor's churches, such as St Anne's,
Limehouse, or St George's-in-the-East, or the dark bulk of
warehouses and the spidery black crane-jibs marking the
River's twisted course; the whole softened by the blue haze
of distance and the brown trails of smoke from funnel and
chimney.

In retrospect that valley of significance, brimming over
with life and surfeited with history, seems always to have
held for me a profound interest and exercised an irresistible
attraction. This, I am willing to admit, may be pure imagination; in those days I was ignorant of the fact that one of my
forbears—not so many generations back—had worked as a
shipwright in the Royal Dockyard in Deptford, had risen to
be foreman, and had then launched out into partnership to
found a small workshop where copper nails and fastenings for
ships were made by hand. That story of Victorian perspicacity
and enterprise was then unknown to me; and I was not even
aware that one of the chimneys smoking away beneath us in
the haze—a little to the east of Greenwich—represented the
outcome of that modest factory in the Deptford High Street

and a monument to my grandfather's acumen and genius. I had yet to learn that I had roots, firmly planted and indisputable, in the soil of that estuary over which we gazed, a bona fide connection with that Thames upon the northern bank of which we lived: a connection that, in years to come, was to be intensified and strengthened until the tides of London River, flowing and ebbing in tireless obedience to the moon, might as well have been the pulse of life itself.

Up there on Observatory Hill we were almost directly opposite St Michael's, and I took a tremendous pride in the belief that we lived exactly on the Greenwich Meridian—the very centre of the world! In support of this assertion I would refer to a cast-iron plaque marking the spot where the Meridian passed through the East India Docks; actually, the church and vicarage must have been a little to the west of it.

The bees hummed in the may-blossom and the flowering chestnuts, heavy sweet scents filled the air, the sound of traffic on the roads or the river barely reached us. I tried clumsily to make a daisy-chain for Nanny who, leaning comfortably against a tree-trunk, read to me from the works of Beatrix Potter or Andrew Lang. Even Mrs Packer's seed-cake tasted better in the open than in the nursery. All too soon it was time to summon the drowsy cabby, trundle away down the hill again, through the Tunnel and back to the hot pavements and unpleasant smells of St Leonard's Road.

But I was really just as happy playing in the dusty Tunnel Gardens; happier on the Brunswick Wharf watching the ships come streaming out of London on the ebb-tide, spelling out their names and struggling to pronounce correctly such words as *Nautilus* and *Eurybates*. Then I was deeply preoccupied in summer with my garden, though, Heaven knows, one got little enough encouragement in Poplar, and my flower-beds were not extensive—perhaps two or three square feet of unproductive London earth, overshadowed by the fence and handicapped from the start by the poisonous drip of plane-trees. Nevertheless, I cultivated them in deadly earnest. Dressed in a brown holland overall reaching well below my calves, button-boots and a large straw hat turned up all round, such as blue-jackets used to wear on tropical stations, I pottered happily for hours among my meagre plants. Little could survive the infertility of the soil or the chemical content of the atmosphere; strange to think that all this flat land near the River had once been the market-garden of London! In the eighteenth-century my mother's family had owned large mulberry-gardens—demanded by the silkworm industry —almost on the spot where we then lived; and Mulberry Street and Dewberry Street commemorated their existence within a stone's throw of the Vicarage.

One year I abandoned horticulture entirely, having been given, for some obscure reason, a book on the rotation of crops, and took up arable farming with enthusiasm, planting rows of wheat and barley instead of flowers. It must have been many years since the soil of East London had been required to produce such a crop! To everyone's surprise, the green blades appeared, but I cannot recall that they ever ripened into ears. In any case, I soon reverted to horticulture and the delights of buying plants in Chrisp Street; for with sixpence, or even ninepence, amassed from one's pocket-money to lay out to the best advantage, one could afford to take one's time, and whichever stall-holder I decided ultimately to patronise would perceive that he had a substantial customer to serve.

The choice was always difficult since the temptations were many: pansies, marigolds, plump red Bachelors' Buttons; an ornamental species of edging plant called Golden Feather, or something of the sort, that I was never able to resist although it was flashy stuff and of no lasting worth; the inevitable lobelias; and asters, which I longed to buy for their bright colours but never did, out of deference to the curious taboo under which they languished in our family. They were said

to have decorated the luncheon-table of the Empress Elizabeth
of Austria immediately before her assassination. This event,
at that time not a very ancient piece of history, had made
little impression upon my mind, but the taboo remained so
strong that even now, in middle age, I can only break it with
misgiving!

To my mother, who came of a family of devoted gardeners,
that wretched plot of ground in Poplar must have been perpetually heartbreaking. Few of my Chrisp Street purchases
survived; even the 'lawn' died away regularly in patches.
There was nothing to be done; it was beyond redemption.
At one end stood the garage, housing my father's Aster car,
a rarity in East London, with its bucket seats, crimson body
and glittering brass carbide lamps. At the other end someone
—either my father or a predecessor—had placed a small
wooden summer-house covered all over with twisted pieces
of 'ornamental' timber, perhaps in a pathetic endeavour to
add a touch of authentic rusticity to the scene. From it, had
one ventured inside to sit upon its seat thickly coated with
soot, a view could be obtained of nothing more rural than the
kitchen windows of the Vicarage and the south transept of
St Michael's. A photograph of that time shows my father
standing in front of the summer-house looking very solemn
and with a volume of Crockford tucked negligently under one
arm, as though he were in the habit of popping in there occasionally for a delightful, quiet browse among those instructive
pages. Actually, it was never used; even our dogs, Scamp and
Jack, did not bother to smell about in it for rats; it was left
severely to itself, and to a species of large, crafty, urban spider
that span particularly grimy webs all over its interior.

In winter-time our only possible outings were to the West
End; and although in those days we could boast a reasonable
steam-train service from South Bromley Station to Broad
Street, there was a great deal of pleasure to be got from riding
on the top of a tram—front seats, if you could get them—

from just outside the Dock Gates up the East India Dock Road and the Commercial Road as far as Aldgate. There would be an unfailing thrill about settling yourself at Nanny's side on the hard wooden seats, which were most uncomfortable but less likely to harbour bugs and fleas. The tram, gathering speed between stops, rocked and roared, and set up a wonderful rolling pitch that made you feel as though you were on the top-deck of a ship. Familiar landmarks, such as the Police Station, St Matthias's Church, the Missions to Seamen and Poplar Town Hall, flashed past with unaccustomed speed, for an electric tram was about the fastest vehicle on the roads in those days. An accepted institution, smooth, clean and comparatively silent, people maintained that those noisy, smelly, unreliable motor-buses could never supersede them. Strangely enough, the horse-tram was only just defunct; I remember being taken to see, as a curiosity, the last one operating in—I think—the Mile End Road.

The passengers were as interesting as the tram-ride: dark-eyed Jewesses with gold ear-rings and shawls; Lascar sailors in blue denims and round red caps; Negroes and Arabs wearing the tarboosh; a coster-woman in her long-fringed shawl and over-feathered hat, thrusting her way on to the tram with a huge basket of flowers, usually artificial but sometimes real ones, such as narcissi, turned an unnatural pink by the simple process of leaving them overnight in a jugful of dye; and stevedores from the Docks, their corduroy trousers bound below the knee with string, their conversation peppered with unusual words which I could not help but overhear. Actually, I heard very little; and from later experience of the London docker I am prepared to believe that they would have curbed their tongues in the presence of a child.

I soon learned not to repeat what I picked up out-of-doors. A workman emerging from an eating-house once burst out furiously: 'By the holy Rood!'—an expression which struck me as so picturesque that, moved by an unwonted desire to shine in front of strangers, I reproduced it at a tea-party in my mother's drawing-room. The shocked faces of the 'aunties' from Lancaster Gate told me at once that I had made a social *gaffe* even before I was removed, chastened and deflated, to the nursery.

Nanny and I made our customary journey by tram on the very morning after the 'Siege of Sidney Street' had ended. In each direction, the driver obligingly crawled at a snail's pace past the end of the sordid little thoroughfare that had become famous overnight. We craned our necks to see a large crowd —the affair had caused a tremendous sensation locally on account of the employment of troops—and a cordon of police-men surrounding the house in which Peter the Painter had held out for so long against the bullets of the soldiers and the will-power of Mr Winston Churchill. It appeared to have every window broken; but even that was not remarkable in Poplar.

By far the most agreeable part of those morning expedi-tions with Nanny—which, to be truthful, extended no further than the City, where we bought paints for my artistic dabblings at a colourman's in Houndsditch—was the obligatory call at an A.B.C. for 'elevenses'. After some persuasion, Nanny allowed me to order 'milk with a dash of coffee'. I was grow-ing up, I felt; after all, at my aunt's I had tasted trifle with sherry in it! The flavour was odd but pleasant; after the first mouthful I had waited for a few moments, fully expecting to experience an extraordinary desire to dance or sing or stagger about—in short, to feel drunk, like the people outside the pubs. Nothing of the sort happened; and I finished my helping with a gratifying sense of sophistication.

The A.B.C., like Shoolbred's, was an estimable establish-ment, but unexciting. I should have liked to lure Nanny into one of the eating-houses in the East India Dock Road—not the Chop Suey dens, for there was something sinister about their frowsy curtained windows—but she would have been horrified: as well take a dose of poison as eat in those places! 'Good Pull Up for Carmen' declared the signs; I had no idea that this was the Edwardian equivalent for 'Ample Parking Space', and I could never imagine why the tempestuous and romantic heroine of Bizet's opera should be expected to patronise them. 'Cut off Joint, Cab, Pots', said the menu scrawled on a slate outside: 'Pudding that Mother Makes'. I forget the prices; but they could have been no more than a few pence for such a meal, at a time when well-known brands of cigarettes were advertised at '10 for 3d'.

Houndsditch and the A.B.C. might be only small beer, but it was a very different matter on those glorious occasions when my father took me 'up West'. From that moment in South Bromley Station when he shook a golden half-sovereign out of his leather purse and asked for 'two first returns to Broad Street', there was no telling what joys could lie ahead. We might go to a cinema—the jerky Westerns made my eyes ache—or Maskelyne and Devant's entrancing entertainment at the St George's Hall. Then the Coliseum had been opened recently by Mr Stoll as a high-class music-hall. He claimed that any member of the most reputable family might see his programmes with profit and enjoyment, and my father and I were proofs positive of the accuracy of his statement. People sometimes looked slightly astonished when I prattled innocently that I had been to 'the music-hall', but the variety acts in the Coliseum bill were superior in both senses of the word. 'Top of the Bill' names were sprinkled liberally throughout the programmes; and if my memory is not at fault, we saw such performers as Hetty King and Ella Shields, in the highest class of male impersonators; Little Tich; Albert Chevalier; the fabulous Lydia Kyasht dancing a *pas de deux* in which she represented a butterfly caught in the net of her partner who, I believe, was none other than Nijinsky; one-act plays performed by West End actors; and once, Sarah Bernhardt herself in a short piece called 'La Vivandière'. It was played in French, and the greatest actress of my time must have been very near the end of her career. I suffered a severe sense of disappointment; perhaps I was too young to be appreciative and she too old to give more than a shadow performance of her supreme talent.

My favourite shows of all were the great spectacular melodramas staged at Drury Lane. In these days, when the mentality of the people has been bound hand and foot and delivered over to the power of the cinema, we are told with condescension that stage-plays such as those wonderful old productions would be failures if they were put on today; that we enjoyed them at all was only because we were so unsophisticated and knew no better in that unenlightened age before the glorious dawn of coloured films and wide screens.

Unfortunately, no one is prepared to put up the money for the purpose of experiment, otherwise I believe that they would prove the domination of celluloid over the field of spectacle to be strangely vulnerable. One tires quickly of the cinema; never of the theatre. Real people are always more intriguing than portraits; they remain longer in the memory. I suppose *The Whip* was the most memorable piece of realistic production ever staged; I certainly found unforgettable— for I can see it still—that incomparably thrilling moment when the famous race-horse, snorting and whinnying with fear, is led down the ramp from his horse-box, rescued in the nick of time just as the great locomotive, hissing with steam, strikes the horse-box in a head-on collision and smashes it to match-wood. I have no idea how it was done; theatre-people believed then in reality rather than illusion, conviction rather than suggestion. The cinema can provide a different brand of thrill, can evoke superlatively many kinds of emotion; but I am prepared to swear it has never achieved quite the equal of that train-smash in *The Whip*.

There is still, to my mind, a special thrill that persists, despite age, time, and the cares of this world, whenever one goes to the play at 'The Lane'. Even its pantomimes seemed to possess a superior glitter, a final magnificence lacking in productions at other theatres, such as the Lyceum, for all that they were of equally inordinate length, and just as lavishly supplied with famous actresses and comedians. For any child, Christmas must represent the highlight of its theatre-going experience; and the tenacious glamour of 'The Lane' must have its origins in those long, exciting, exhausting Boxing Day afternoons, deeply rooted in the heat and stuffiness of the theatre, the smell of oranges from the pit, and that unsurpassable moment, as intoxicating as wine, when the footlights go up and the houselights go down!

Then, Christmas without *Peter Pan* would have been comparable to one's Christmas dinner without the pudding; and again, I cannot remember the time when I was not familiar with the Darling family, Nana, the dearly-loved Smee, the hated Captain Hook, Tinker Bell and the rest. Although we took instantly to *Where the Rainbow Ends*—which I have been surprised to discover was first produced as late as 1911 —it never managed to transmit the same quality of seasonable magic. Despite the Hans Andersen flavour of the scene where the trees come to life, the feeling of the play took us out of the nursery into the schoolroom: it encouraged the more adult emotion of patriotism. Nevertheless, the moment when St George—looking neither saintly nor archaic, but rather like a typical naval officer participating in the local pageant— is revealed in all his shining armour is a superb one. We shouted ourselves hoarse, and would have smacked with enthusiasm the head of any German who dared to make derogatory remarks just then; for already we had come insensibly to regard them as our natural enemies.

Also in the year 1911, when I was eight years old and a seasoned theatre-goer, Max Reinhardt brought to London his revolutionary and amazing spectacle, *The Miracle*.

I should explain at once that, if you liked *The Miracle* at all, you became infatuated by it; it was like a drug; you could not stay away; and Olympia, previously associated in my mind with motor shows, which were dull, fatiguing, and dominated by a frightening rubber giant advertising a certain make of tyre, suddenly became a sort of Mecca set in the prosaic deserts of West Kensington.

I saw nine performances of *The Miracle*; my father, I believe, had some extra evening attendances to his credit. Humperdinck's haunting and inspired music was irresistible. I would hum and whistle nothing else; 'Carmen' and 'The Yeoman of the Guard' were ousted instantly from the foremost place in my musical affections. On one rapturous occasion we found ourselves travelling home from Olympia in the District Railway with the leader of the orchestra; before leaping from the train at Earl's Court he drew five lines rapidly on the back of an old envelope and scribbled thereon the Spielmann's *motif*—heard at the end of every scene whenever he has gained another soul for evil—which we found to be correct in every note when eventually we were able to buy the full score.

The stage management was masterly. Before the performances began, boys dressed as acolytes in scarlet cassocks walked round and round the perimeter of that vast arena swinging censers, from which clouds of incense streamed perpetually up to vanish into the dim arc of the roof. An illusion was thus at once created, which enwrapped you as soon as you came in, of mysticism, reverence, and even of devotion. It was not difficult to imagine that you were seated in the transept of a great cathedral, that you were part of a huge, silent congregation, watching through the blue, misty, aromatic atmosphere the enactment by nuns, choristers and peasants of those strange and intricate religious ceremonies.

Complete darkness had to be introduced for some moments before the performance began; then a shaft of coldly impersonal, pallid light shone down, as though from a clerestory window, upon the plaster-white and motionless statue of the Madonna, crowned with gold, robed in gorgeous colours: the curtain had risen on that simple story which, reduced to essentials, was nothing more nor less than a drama of the eternal conflict continuing within us all between the flesh and the spirit.

The impact of *The Miracle* upon my finer susceptibilities was resounding. For a time I wavered in my desire to go to sea, temporarily seduced by my wish to become a nun—not that I had the least glimmering of a vocation nor the faintest conception of a conventual existence—and for months after the production had ceased my sister and I played out the principal scenes during school holidays, taking turn and turn about to be the Madonna—in a red quilt and car board crown, perched uncomfortably on the brass footrail of the spare-room bed—or the Nun, in a black coat of my mother's and a confirmation veil, kneeling in an attitude of pious adoration before the old ottoman in which we kept our toys. The next Naval and Military Tournament seemed almost a desecration of that dedicated arena!

En famille we would visit the White City, where by ascending in the fabulous Flip-Flap we viewed the whole of London from an unprecedented height. With my scholarly mother as mentor, I grew familiar with such serious-minded haunts as the British Museum, or heard Evensong sung in St Paul's Cathedral. But, as usual, it was in my father's company that the most exciting, the most delightful and grown-up experiences took place. Sometimes he would take me out to lunch, invariably at the Holborn Restaurant, which until recently stood on the corner of Kingsway. He would eat nowhere else; it was, he declared, the only place that he could afford at which the food was good, the air fresh, and the tables far enough apart to give you plenty of elbow-room; and it was here that I first learned my way about a menu written in French, and not to be taken unawares when the waiter pushed in my chair, or spread my table napkin, with a Latin flourish, upon my knees.

Any entertainment or excursion devised by my father pleased me to perfection. That small gold coin, scarcely larger than a sixpence, proffered by him and accepted by the grimy hand of the booking-clerk at South Bromley Station, might have been our entrance-money to a vast and immensely superior pleasure-ground, for London in those days was a most agreeable place to move about in. No one had ever heard of a queue; you could walk along the pavements comfortably without having to push, or being pushed; and there were no noticeable foreigners. The town, I suppose, was comparatively empty: a mere four million people lived there, and there were few excursions, few invading armies from the suburbs. You had to be wary of the traffic when crossing the streets, but given reasonable care it was possible to cross almost anywhere without much waiting. Only the crossing-sweepers, in their smartly-cockaded hats, could dart with impunity under the very wheels of vehicles in the prosecution of their task. I hesitate to assess the growing ratio of motor cars in London then, for we rode in hansoms, rather than in taxi-cabs: a smooth and pleasant method of propulsion. As in a rickshaw, you sat high above ground-level, and saw everything that was going on; but in a rickshaw you are conscious of the over-taxed, if willing, sinews of a sweating coolie, whereas in a hansom you were aware only of the horse's powerful hindquarters drawing you apparently with perfect ease.

There were still plenty of horse-buses. People used to say: 'Don't ride in those motor-bus contraptions—they're always breaking down!' After that, I was frightened of them, imagining that they 'broke down' quite literally, into a heap of fragments. Besides, it was exhilarating to travel on the top of a horse-bus high up behind the driver, watching him as he handled the reins so expertly, cracked his whip, or applied his huge hand-brake. You went along at a good pace, too, for there were no traffic-lights to stop you and no traffic-jams, either, except at such notorious spots as the Bank Corner, over which grown-ups were already shaking their heads and saying that something must be done. Naturally, you were exposed to all the elements; but people did not consider that so intolerable as they do today. There were oil-cloth covers to pull up and fasten round you when it rained, although they did little more than keep your lap dry.

The Underground was my favourite mode of transport, above all in winter. The warm gales blowing through its labyrinths, the curious sharp smell, the fascination of its trains running like illuminated, mechanised worms deep under the earth's surface, never failed to intrigue me. I longed for the day when I should be grown-up and able to ride to my heart's content on the Central and the Bakerloo, or round and round the Inner Circle. I would know all the stations without having to refer to the little maps; and to demonstrate my independence, I would buy large brown-paper bags full of ripe, white-heart cherries—everything is far more enjoyable when enlivened by something to eat—to refresh me on my perpetual circumnavigation of the London Tube.

12. Poplar Pavements

THE figures, drawn in varying degrees of clarity, of my
parents, my sister, Nanny, the curates, and our household,
compose the foreground of this childhood scene; and behind
them, against the monotonous pattern of the streets and
houses, move the shadowy people of the town itself. But not
always shadowy and by no means always drab. On a fine Bank
Holiday, especially at Easter and Whitsun, the favoured
season for weddings, all the colours of the spectrum could be
seen parading outside St Michael's. Everyone walked to their
wedding, for there was little enough cash to spare for such
a luxury as a carriage: you saved it for your funeral, when
you had no choice but to ride!

First the groom would appear, a dazed lout awkward in
his Sunday black or grey, an enormous buttonhole flaunting
strangely on the sober cloth of his jacket, a clean white
kerchief folded round his throat, a new cap set gingerly upon
his well-oiled hair. His grinning companions hung back
uncomfortably at the porch; they had probably never been
inside a church before and were shy of the unfamiliar sur-

roundings, as they were unaccustomed to a day of leisure and their best clothes.

Round the corner next would sweep the bride and her party. On this great day of her life she had crammed as much colour as possible into her attire, as though to compensate, poor thing, for all the years ahead that she would spend in drab working-clothes. The style was always the same: a long, tight-waisted dress, fashionably cut with leg-o'-mutton sleeves, boned, lace-edged high collars, ruchings, flounces, deep hems of velvet and all. It was the colours that were so startling; they seemed to prefer an aching violet, vivid royal blue, the sort of pink that is now called 'shocking', a brilliant emerald green. On their puffed-out, padded *coiffures* were perched the huge cartwheel hats worn in those days by coster-girls and countesses alike, with this difference, that the coster-girls overdid the feathers, which vied with the dresses in the violence of their colouring. Long ear-rings of paste or glass hung from their ears and paste ornaments glittered in their hair. They were magnificently overpowering, these fine, buxom women, tightly laced into their bright clothes, the great plumes of pink, blue, green and purple nodding and tossing on their handsome heads!

The bridesmaids wore much the same style of dress, if naturally less splendid in order not to detract from the glories of the bride. As they bunched up their long skirts carefully to cross the road—the crossing-sweepers, too, had a day off, and the carriage-way was soon befouled—you could see their feet and ankles encased in high, lace-up boots with pointed toes. A constant procession of such parties disappeared into the church, where my father and his curates would spend the entire day marrying couples as fast as they could, until the prescribed hour of three o'clock after which marriage-ceremonies could not be performed. To get them 'done' in time, they were often obliged to deal with several couples at once, standing in a long row at the chancel steps.

Constrained, shy and awkward during the ceremony itself, they would become too confused to tell right hand from left. If they were seafaring bridegrooms, my father could sometimes straighten out the tangle by saying: 'Take her port hand in your starboard one!'

But the flimsy bonds of decorum would burst with ease as soon as they had emerged into the open air once more. Shrill peals of feminine laughter and the hoarse guffaws of the men demonstrated the relief from unaccustomed strain. The happy couples and their friends gathered for a while outside the west door, where the usual pelting with rice and confetti redoubled the shrieks. But the groups soon separated; most, without any beating about the bush, went straight as arrows for the nearest public-house; they had no distance to go. Occasionally there was a small, pathetic scene, a tiny struggle of wills on the pavement outside. Maybe the bride's family had arranged, at considerable sacrifice, to entertain the wedding-guests at home, and the bridegroom had agreed to what had seemed an admirable plan. But passing the pub would be his undoing, especially when he had a pocket full of money for the honeymoon. The place would be packed to the doors, and the agreeable roar of boozy conversation, the smell of beer and spirits wafting out upon the warm air, would be too much for his good resolutions. Time and time again I watched the little exhibition of weakness, the arguments, the tugging at a reluctant arm, the flaring-up of tempers, the inevitable 'words'. In the end the easiest solution seemed to be for everyone to go amicably together into the 'boozer'. Hours later they would emerge in varying stages of intoxication, and the day presumably ended in the familiar pattern, to which there seemed to be no alternative, of quarrels, nausea, empty pockets, fuddled heads, and final insensibility.

Memory does not need the aid of statistics to prove that drunkenness was far more prevalent than it is today. Wages were low, but drink was cheap. Of an earlier generation it used to be said that a gin-addict could get drunk for three-pence and dead-drunk for fourpence, the latter tariff including clean straw to sleep it off on! To give the devil his due, there was not very much else, even in my day, on which to spend your money. Cinemas were few, smelly 'flea-pits' with flicker-ing films that made your head ache; there were no greyhound tracks, and whippet racing was said to be on the decline; no radio programmes, no television; and a day at Southend was the height of anyone's ambition as an outing. There was football on Saturdays—but no pools—and there were music-halls: locally the Queen's in Poplar High Street, and not so very far away the famous Stratford Empire, at which all the favourites topped the bill in turn. The People's Palace had not long been opened in the Mile End Road, but I doubt whether it had yet acquired a regular clientèle. Apart from that, there were the public-houses, open seven days a week and practically eighteen hours out of the twenty-four.

My father, who regarded drunkenness as one of the major problems in his parish, endeavoured to counter it by preaching temperance rather than total abstinence, although teetotalism was in all probability an easier target for his parishioners, who were often lacking grievously in will-power. He himself was no blue-ribbonite; he enjoyed good wine, kept a case of beer in the house and also a wicker-covered demijohn of whisky, which cost a sum so modest as to be scarcely credible to the tax-ridden generations of today. You could buy a proprietary brand at that time for three shillings and sixpence a bottle.

A docker who had come to see my father noticed the demi-john and asked what it was. On being told that it contained whisky, his eyes opened very wide and he wanted to know how long it lasted.

'Oh—four or five months—it all depends,' said my father.

' 'Strewth!' exclaimed the docker. 'If it was me, I'd drain

it to the last drop as soon as look at it! Couldn't abear to keep it in the 'ouse and not touch it. I dunnow 'ow you does it, guv'nor, honest I don't!'

However, as my father truly maintained, they hardly ever drank themselves to death for the simple reason that they could not afford it. But drink was so often at the bottom of the minor tragedies, the inability to keep a job, the perennial visits to the pawn-shop, the sold-up homes. The habitual wife-beaters were generally habitual drunkards, too; and sometimes the tragedy overstepped the bounds and became a full catastrophe.

On a fine morning in early summer when people, even in Poplar, should have felt thankful to be alive, my father received an urgent summons. In the squalid back-kitchen of a house, no better and certainly no worse than most, he faced a stark admission of defeat: defeat for himself and for the faith he taught no less than for the vanquished. The body of the housewife, small, thin, old beyond her years, swung with a hideous levity from a hook in the ceiling. My father cut it down instantly and sent the husband, fuddled equally with drink and shock, for the doctor; but it was, of course, too late. The husband was quite unrepentant; and if he was upset, it was solely on account of the inconvenience she had caused him. It was Derby Day, he reminded my father, and he had meant to go to Epsom. His wife, as usual, had spoilt all that.

'Spiteful to the last,' declared the aggrieved man. 'She's gorn and 'anged 'erself wiv the rope I does up me picnic 'amper wiv. Messed up me 'ole day, she 'as. She knows I'm a delicate-minded bloke and wouldn't like to use it arter that!'

Answering another urgent call, my father found the ambulance already at the door of the house. The young wife and the baby to which she had given birth in the small hours were being rushed to hospital; the mother had had a severe internal hæmorrhage, and it was doubtful whether she would live. The hæmorrhage, the midwife grimly explained, had been brought on because the husband had thrashed her. Inured to brutalities, even my father could hardly believe his ears. The husband, a sullen young brute, was resentful and bewildered. Evidently he felt the need to justify himself.

'She wouldn't get up,' he complained. 'She wouldn't get up and cook my dinner. ' 'Ow was I to know she was feelin' bad? I comes back from work and wants me dinner. She wouldn't get up, the lazy bitch!'

And yet it was amongst these people that there flourished, despite the hardships, the squalor, the despair and the sickness, qualities of charity and courage such as my father was not to find so easily among those whose lot lay in kinder circumstances. Over and over again they proved themselves to be more neighbourly, more selflessly good to those in trouble, more patient and stoical in suffering than any in his experience either then or later.

It is manifestly unfair to blame drink for every act of physical and mental cruelty. Other contributory factors were many and inevitable: bad working conditions, atrocious housing, precarious employment, extremes of poverty and disease. Sweating, for instance, was still practised by the wholesale garment-manufacturers, and a widow in the parish told my father that she was paid one shilling and eightpence for one dozen finished shirts—a good employer, too, for he supplied the sewing cotton! She was obliged to work far into the night in order to earn a bare livelihood, and her eyes were red and swollen with overstrain. Dock-strikes were frequent; the men were struggling to emerge from the deplorable conditions of their employment, whereby they fought amongst themselves at the dock-gates to catch the 'caller's' eye and gain a half-day's labour. And the death-rate was still far too high, especially that rate of child mortality which had so perturbed my mother, even if it had receded from the shocking peak of Mayhew's day.

I can certainly testify to the frequency of funerals in our

parish, for I watched every one of them from my nursery windows, although I regarded them as considerably less inviting than the weddings, and far inferior in entertainment value to the drunks. They attracted plenty of spectators; and I thought it odd that a person at whom no one would have bothered to look when alive should be the magnet of so many eyes when he, or she, had become nothing but an empty shell (as I had been taught) shut up in a wooden box. People turned out of the pubs to watch a funeral go by, especially that of a child: the smaller the coffin, the louder the exclamations of pity and sorrow, the more frequent the raising of a hand to dash away a tear. Nevertheless, 'respect for the dead' was not an empty phrase in Poplar, for scarcely a man omitted to doff his cap as the hearse passed him: a gentle act of courtesy and reverence that a present generation seems to have discarded, either through scepticism, ignorance, or sheer oafishness, of which even a London loafer could not then have been accused.

I dare say the publicans appreciated the stimulus of a funeral; everyone would feel obliged to return to the bar for another drink in memory of the late departed, or even just to steady the nerves after such a gloomy reminder of the mutability of human affairs. Besides, there would be the whole turn-out to be discussed and criticised, for in such matters the measure of one's wealth and importance was, as usual, quantity: the number of carriages, the number of wreaths, the number of hideous black ostrich feathers nodding from the heads of the horses and the roof of the hearse.

This terrible *pompe funèbre* achieved its desired effect of solemnity and sombre grief. The flowers were often artificial, and the Cockney, obeying the dictates of strict economy and realism, frequently invested in a tasteless arrangement of waxen blooms under a glass dome, guaranteed to produce a professional atmosphere of bogus sorrow combined with parsimony at any graveside. The wreaths of fresh flowers were highly ornate, plain circles being outnumbered easily by harps, empty chairs, angels' wings, anchors—undoubtedly a sea connection here—and a pair of floral gates representing 'the Gates of Heaven opening wide for thee', this last being an easy favourite.

Out of the carriage windows peered the faces of the mourners, if not tear-stained, at least dutifully composed in decorous expressions of woe, although at times they could not restrain a flicker of gratification at being seen by the neighbours riding grandly in a carriage and sweeping, as proudly as the Lord Mayor of London himself, right round the open space in front of the Vicarage before drawing up at the church. Nobody ever dreamed of not wearing mourning, even if it had to be bought on tick; the womenfolk were often as heavily draped in crinkly black crêpe as any Continental widow; in the hand, almost immobilised by unaccustomed pressure of a black kid glove, would be clutched a hand-kerchief with an inch-wide mourning border. The funeral mutes wore generous 'weepers' round the crowns of their shabby and somewhat moth-eaten-looking top-hats, but their shoes were often cracked and the shoulders of their ill-fitting frock-coats faded to a distressingly unmistakable shade of green. The horses, on the other hand, were of a wonderfully uniform and glossy ebony, due, we were always given to understand, to the generous application of black boot-polish. A local undertaker who neglected this simple expedient and allowed his beasts to reveal a brownish patina or a patch of grey soon went out of business. Black horses were *de rigueur* at funerals, and if you paid for a black horse—through the nose, too—you had a right to expect a horse that *was* black from the tip of his muzzle to the longest hair in his tail.

The funereal plumes, strapped singly to each horse's head and sprouting in a gruesome grove above the hearse, I could not bear. If a cortège passed us closely in the street, I would shrink back fearfully against the house-fronts. I imagined that spirits—not the spirits of the dead, but evil spirits, demons, emissaries of Satan—lurked amongst those ghoulish, fluttering black fronds which seemed to be inviting you to join them as they nodded and becked in a horribly animated manner. And Satan, to me in those days, was a very real and living person; I had never set eyes on him, but I was very sure that he existed; moreover, I knew well enough that I should see him were I so unwise as to look for him in certain places at a certain time.

Inside the church he could not go, and I doubted whether he dared set foot within the precincts of the Vicarage, sufficiently hallowed—I hoped—by the proximity of St Michael's, the benign influence of several successive vicars, and the additional effect of the innumerable curates, churchwardens, district visitors and other virtuous persons who frequented it daily. But his haunts were obvious: certain dark, sinister and noisome alleys, in which I had a notion he would like to loiter about the hour of sunset, and a huge, sooty brick cavern, to be seen from the high viaduct near Broad Street Station, where, in the dim gleams thrown by a few scattered electric-light bulbs, daemonic forms toiled away at some obscure task, far below the earth's surface and in perpetual gloom. The place was probably a goods depot belonging to the railway; yet I had a shrewd suspicion that it was an entrance to Hell itself, conveniently situated for the devil to use when he wanted to come sneaking about Poplar after the souls of my father's parishioners. But, of course, once having been an angel, he knew how to fly; and on moonlight nights I hesitated to look out once the curtains had been drawn, for fear that I might see that black figure with eyes like red-hot coals, its cloak outspread like a huge bat winging its way above the unfortunate roofs of Bromley-by-Bow.

As a rule, there were many more funerals in the winter, except when a sudden epidemic swept through the densely over-crowded river-side parishes. Such outbreaks usually occurred in a hot, dry summer, when the town began to smell, the River ran low, and the heavy exhalations of dirt, refuse, mud, of unwashed bodies and the rancid cooking-fat of cheap eating-houses and fried fish shops hung like a miasma over the sweltering streets. Once at least there was a small-pox scare, for I can recall the pride with which I displayed a scarlet ribbon on my vaccinated arm.

As soon as the weather turned hot—and in retrospect, so many of the summers seem to have been very hot indeed—hawkers appeared at the kerbside with little wooden stands holding large tumblers of bright-coloured waters purporting to be 'cool fruit drinks, penny a glass'. There would be lemon, and orange, and a vivid pink liquid called 'sarsaparilla', which was the general favourite. Since the vendors carried no ice, and bits of straw, chaff from the horses' nose-bags, grit and dust from the road, all whirling together on the hot summer breeze, could blow into them without let or hindrance, the drinks were certainly not cool, and extremely unhygienic; but people, especially women and children, bought them thirstily.

The Italian ice-cream sellers turned up as well, in their little pony-drawn carts, sheltered by red and white striped awnings and painted with elaborate flower designs. Wherever they stopped a crowd of ragged children collected, if only in the hope that someone more affluent than they might generously 'spare a copper'. Ice-cream was a luxury to me; I don't suppose I tasted it more than twice a year, at Christmas and on my annual birthday pilgrimage to the Zoo. I longed to buy the halfpenny cornets and penny slabs that looked so tempting, but Nanny would have been horrified if I had done so. She believed firmly that ice-cream was practically lethal unless made by some firm of repute such as Gunter's or Buszard's; and the Italians were said to concoct the stuff at home, keeping it, for some extraordinary reason, under their beds in wash-tubs! The mere idea was quite enough to make one squeamish.

Since there were so few playgrounds and the swarming children of the district were obliged to play in the streets, I could not fail to become familiar with their favourite games. These varied little, and appeared to be ruled by strict seasonal conventions. In winter, when a warming form of exercise was needed, they whipped tops, bowled hoops, and skipped with tireless energy. In summer, when the pavements were less likely to be muddy, they played marbles and chalked out hop-scotch squares. The little girls nursed dolls, none the less cherished for being shapeless lumps of rag or wood, dressed carefully in soiled scraps of shabby finery. The little boys trundled each other and their baby brothers and sisters about in carts constructed from an old packing-case resting precariously upon a pair of discarded pram-wheels, while the older boys roller-skated ceaselessly.

A curious kind of bush-telegraph appeared to exist among the children over their games. On a given day, for no obvious reason but as though by magic, the hop-scotch squares vanished from the pavements, the tops and hoops emerged from their long summer rest—and in the autumn, vice versa. Who made the decision to change from one set of games to another, and how it was spread so rapidly from street to street, indeed, from parish to parish, was a minor mystery upon which no light was ever shed, although Nanny and I would remark on it regularly twice a year.

Skipping was a game evidently considered suitable at any season. It was particularly popular with girls, who practised it so assiduously that they achieved considerable skill in such variations as double-skipping, cross-skipping, and the universal 'vinegar, salt and pepper'. Making fast one end of the rope to a convenient lamp-post, a girl would begin to turn it while her companions, one after the other, would join in skipping to its slow rhythm. Jump in, Ada!' they would exhort each other as the pace of the rope quickened. 'Jump in, May!' And Ada and Mary squealing with excitement, would jump in, followed by their playmates until there were too many for the rope, or it was turning too fast; then someone would catch a foot, stumble, and the game would end in confusion and shrieks of laughter.

This form of multiple skipping was indulged in by grownups as well, but curiously enough, only on one day in the year. On Good Friday, when the streets were empty of traffic, parties of men and women dressed in their holiday clothes would move slowly along, skipping as they went. The long rope, held at each end by a man who walked sideways while he turned it, stretched right across the street. Men and women 'jumped in' like the children, sometimes singly, often in pairs facing each other, their arms round each other's waists. At times the holders of the rope called out plaintively for someone to relieve them while they took a turn at skipping themselves. Generally they were decorous, even solemn, in their behaviour, as though performing a rite, but later in the day, when they had visited a few public-houses, there would be a good deal of hilarity and horse-play. Try as I might, I cannot associate this curious spectacle with any other Bank Holiday in the year, neither can I proffer any explanation, unless it was the last obscure manifestation of an ancient custom.

With all the ingenuity and aplomb so typical of the Cockney, those hardy dockland children surely extracted every particle of entertainment from the meagre facilities afforded by the streets—if you can describe a lamp-post, a kerbstone, a paling, as facilities. They sprang in hordes, apparently from the pavements, whenever anything in the least out of the ordinary occurred, a category ranging from a street-accident—comparatively rare in those motorless days—or the arrival of an ambulance to remove a sick person from a house, to that unhappy sight, all too common during a sharp winter, of a fallen horse.

Always morbidly, perhaps unreasonably, sensitive to the

sufferings of animals, I pitied the poor beasts slipping and straining to keep on their legs as they drew the heavy wagons and drays to and from the Docks, while the carters thrashed them on with furious shouts. I could not bear to see the whiplash curling round their smoking hindquarters, and used to pray fervently at night that the horses might be spared and the carters punished. I dreaded to see them down on the ground, their flanks heaving, steam from their bodies rising in clouds on the bitter air, the coats matted and dark with sweat, an expression of patient pleading in the rolling eye as though to say: 'I've done enough—let me be.'

'Come on! There's an 'orse dahn!' People ran quickly, collected like magic round the fallen beast; one of the free shows of London—don't miss it! They watched with callous, closed faces the unlucky creature's struggle to rise. Someone would sit on the horse's head, or put a sack over it, which was said to make it easier to get them on their feet again. But it seemed to me that a great deal of straining and hauling, of thrashing and kicking and cruel jerking at the bridle was necessary before the unhappy animal was up. It would stand quivering slightly, nostrils distended, the breath coming from them in spurts of white smoke: the picture of harassed dejection. I do not know why we ever stopped to watch the sorry spectacle; I always had to be led away in floods of tears, a reaction seldom produced by the more frequent sight of a child being cuffed, kicked, or beaten with the buckle end of a belt. *That* merely made me feel sick, and inexplicably ashamed; and I am not alone, I fancy, in this varying degree of susceptibility which is, however, not so simple to define.

Cruelty to children is unforgivable enough—the cruelty of one human soul to another—but the child, for all its physical helplessness, can speak, can communicate its torment, summon aid, and even run away. But cruelty to animals is doubly unpardonable: as a lesser form of creation they have been put in the charge, so to speak, of *homo sapiens*, and yet find themselves the victims of a misplaced trust, the prisoners of those superior beings to whom they should be able to look for something better than the expedient ferocities of the animal world—which after all, are usually inseparable from the primitive instinct of self-preservation. There is a moving dignity about the patience, the resignation with which a beast endures the treatment it must suffer at the hands of man.

All this was beyond my youthful powers of reasoning; but it did occur to me that, to be logical, I should become a vegetarian . . . if the prospect of a staple diet composed of Mrs Packer's soggy cabbage had not filled me with revulsion. Then I was worried by the idea that one has no means of measuring the amount of pain that can be inflicted on a mosquito, a wasp, an earthworm—even the fleas that we caught occasionally when riding on the trams and which were so firmly put to death by Nanny. Perhaps, after all, the Jains were the only people with the true solution.

. The draught-horse has practically vanished from the London streets, its hardships and sufferings put an end to by the internal combustion engine. Like the ceremonial skipping on Good Friday—which must long have lapsed by now—it will soon be one of the forgotten fragments of the past, and the clop-clop of its hooves will shortly follow the cries of street-sellers into perpetual silence.

We heard but few street-cries in Poplar, for the luxury-trades do not waste their time in poverty-stricken districts such as ours, where people seldom had so much as a penny to spare for a bunch of violets in the spring. Our hawkers dealt in goods of a strictly practical nature, and most frequently to be heard were the raucous yells of the rag-and-bone man, the 'any-old-iron' man, the firewood-and-bricket seller, and the long-drawn, unmelodious wail of the cats' meat woman as she came daily down St Leonard's Road with her basket of repellent scraps on her arm and a string of mewing cats behind her.

Bundled up in rusty black shawls, there used to be an old woman who chirped away hoarsely at the kerbside: 'Groundsel for the dickie-birds—buy my groundsel, dearie—fresh groundsel for the dickie-birds!'

I hope they, too, have disappeared for ever, those poor 'dickie-birds', the commonest pets of East London: the thrushes, blackbirds, finches and linnets, immured for life in a tiny cage in which they could never stretch their wings, hung on a backyard wall with no more than a few square feet of sky to stare at through the one open side of the cage. I used to dream that I had enough money to buy up and set free every single cage-bird in the whole of Poplar; indeed, I seriously considered it once, on getting the fabulous tip of ten gold sovereigns from a generous godfather. People said: 'You mustn't be so soft-hearted! They would be frightened to death if they were turned loose—or mobbed to death by other birds.' I still cherished my dream; it seemed to me far better to die in freedom than to exist in such confinement. If you called to them as you passed, they fluttered their cramped wings a little, piped up bravely a note or two which soon trailed away into silence. Motionless, the beady dark eye stared back at you inquiringly as though to ask: 'Why do you come here to plague me, you earthbound mortal, who are free to walk away yourself, and yet have denied me for ever the right to the skies?' This distress at seeing animals or birds confined was always sharp with me, like a physical discomfort, and would mar quite seriously the birthday visit to the Zoo.

In early evening the paper-boys came bawling down the street. In lieu of radio sets and newsreels, they brought us the first tidings of the world's events.

'Hark!' Nanny would exclaim. 'What's that they're calling?'

'Great London fire!' 'Famous statesman dies!' 'Mine disaster—many dead!' they cried, and passed on out of hearing.

215

My mother would recount how she first heard the news of Mafeking as a distant murmur travelling westward over London—she was then at Lancaster Gate—and growing in volume until it became a deafening roar, the news-boys racing as fast as their legs could carry them, shouting until their lungs were near to bursting, while people snatched the papers from their hands and cheered as they stood in the streets, as they had not done for months—the Relief of Mafeking!

I did not expect ever to have so exciting an experience as that, for people said that nations were too civilised to go to war any more; but once at least I heard that strange sound of news literally spreading itself abroad. A General Election was in progress—something that I connected vaguely with the electric light until its significance was explained to me— amid a welter of adult conversation in which the two subjects of Tariff Reform and Home Rule were discussed unceasingly. Indeed, they seemed to have been talking about both of them ever since I had first become conscious of what grown-ups said to each other. Their meaning was beyond my comprehension; but I knew that we were still governed—apparently very badly—by the Liberals, who were as stupid as they were dishonest. But on this occasion—it may have been the first General Election of 1910—Bow and Bromley returned a Unionist, probably the last Tory to represent the constituency, for Mr George Lansbury got in at the second election; and it was the news of the Conservative victory, accompanied by cheering and booing, that I heard moving steadily towards us—this time from the west—like a rising storm of wind and rain. An alarming sound; but a great deal more dramatic and more human than the measured tones of the news-reader, trained to be impersonal, falling flatly upon a quiet room from the blank face of a receiving-set.

Of all the street-cries, I had a favourite. On a foggy, raw, mid-January day, when the bitter pall of winter hung drearily over the houses, when the eye could rest on nothing that was

not dark, or drab, or dismal, the cheerful bell of the muffin
man was heard drawing near. Here he came, swinging down
the street, tray on head, bell in hand, making no concession
to the cold beyond a muffler round his throat, as though the
good cheer of his wares was quite enough to warm him.
Summoned by Nanny's imperious waving from the nursery
window, he would swing the tray down off his head with
practised ease, whip off a clean white cloth and display the
piles of muffins. Sometimes I would be allowed to go downstairs and ask him for twopennyworth. By now I have
forgotten whether they cost a halfpenny or a farthing each;
but the four, or the eight, would be carefully selected and
carried triumphantly indoors. Toasted at the nursery fire and
buttered thickly, how they glorified nursery tea and even
improved the flavour of Mrs Packer's fearsome cakes! I swear
there are no such muffins made today!

But of all the sounds that echoed along our streets and
drifted in at the Vicarage windows, there was one for which
I listened eagerly and heard with pleasure and excitement;
a sound so common then, but now preserved merely as a
museum-piece: the notes of a barrel-organ. The gay rattle
of those insouciant tones must fall upon the ears of the present
generation as a sound both artificial and archaic, very much
as we in our generation heard the thin, thready tunes of our
great-aunt's musical-box. For us, the barrel-organ evokes a
shameless sentimentality, a blatant nostalgia; it summons up
the very essence of childhood, of that calm lake, reflecting a
sunny sky so seldom marred by clouds, upon which one
drifted first before venturing on the tide-rips, the rapids, the
heavy seas and hidden rocks of life's difficult navigation.

We had our own special organ-grinder, who visited us at
regular weekly intervals. He was listened to with uncritical
appreciation; and after he had played his repertoire—which
we soon got to know by heart—we would run downstairs
and give him our pennies. He tied a coloured handkerchief

round his head and carried a monkey in a red velvet jacket, but for all that I fancy he was a Cockney; organ-grinders were expected to be Italian, just as street-musicians had to be German. Sometimes a pirate would poach on his preserves, to our unqualified delight, for we would have welcomed a barrel-organ recital every day of the week; besides, we heard some different tunes into the bargain. And often on our walks we would come across an organ playing down a side-turning, surrounded by an audience of enraptured children, the little girls holding out the torn skirts of their dresses and pointing their bare, muddy toes as though they were all ballerinas in embryo.

It must be almost impossible for the modern child, apathetic to the point of boredom with a surfeit of broadcast concerts, portable gramophones and radio sets, television at home and in the school, to realise how starved we were of music. I was especially fortunate: in addition to my splendid gramophone with its crimson horn and a handle to wind it up with, my mother played for us occasionally on the grand piano in the drawing-room, and my father, at the upright in his study, did his best to teach us the cream of Grand Opera and Gilbert and Sullivan.

As for that marvel of the Edwardian age, the pianola, it performed a major part in my musical education. When wheeled up to the study piano and loaded with a perforated music-roll, it would play for you with mechanical virtuosity for just as long as you had the energy to work its pedals. By means of the various little buttons and handles along its front you could adjust the tempo, achieving dramatic *rallentandos* or *allegrettos;* or operate the loud pedal, although for a really impressive *crescendo* you had to pump very hard at it indeed. By the end of the Tannhauser Overture or Elgar's 'Pomp and Circumstance', or the last movement of Beethoven's Fifth Symphony, I would be crimson in the face with heat and excitement.

Large orchestral works reduced to the terms of a single pianoforte may have offended the susceptibilities of the *cognoscenti*, but it was an excellent method of familiarising you thoroughly with the themes and structure of the classic masterpieces. My father took me to hear *Carmen* at Covent Garden when I was about six years old, and two ladies in the seats behind us who had been delivering themselves of scathing comments on the absurdity of bringing so young a child to hear Grand Opera, were disconcertingly reduced to silence when I exclaimed with a horrid precocity at the end of the Overture: 'Oh, Daddy, the Death Motif!'

Privileged as I was through the good fortune of having musical parents, there were even so few enough opportunities of hearing music of any sort, good or bad, light or classical. For the latest popular songs we had to depend on the whistling of errand-boys, since there was a decided time-lag before such ditties reached the cylinders of the barrel-organs, and it was upon them, after all, that we relied for our up-to-date tunes. Their repertoires usually included an operatic piece, such as the famous duet from *Il Trovatore* or the *Cavalleria* Intermezzo; and, of course, a musical comedy selection, for this was the golden age of musical comedy and the choice was wide: *The Country Girl, Miss Hook of Holland, The Cingalee*, and many more. Waltzes were our great favourites; Nanny and I knew them well—'Gold and Silver', 'The Blue Danube', 'After the Ball', 'The Merry Widow', and the very latest ones of all, considered slightly modernistic, 'In the Shadows' and 'Destiny'. The crisp rhythm of a waltz comes out very well in the staccato touch of a barrel-organ, especially when adorned with all sorts of elaborate trills, grace-notes and runs put in for good measure by the 'orchestrators'. But for sheer virtuosity and dramatic effect you want to hear the instrument at full volume playing patriotic songs and marches, such as something by de Souza, or 'Soldiers of the Queen' and 'Land of Hope and Glory'. This last would arouse in me such imperial fervour that I would stamp round and round the nursery table, my chest puffed out with martial pride and yelling 'Make thee mi—ightier yet!' until Nanny would tell me to be quiet for goodness sake!

The scent of apples in a loft, of bean-flowers, hay; the smell of certain spices and a special wood burned in cooking-fires; the conglomerate ship-smells of fuel-oil, paint, mixed cargoes, and varnished wood warm in the sun: these things are perceptibly more evocative of a time and a place than sights or even sounds. Alas! The smells of East London were not such as one would wish to recall. To re-create most perfectly in my mind the dingy purlieus of Poplar and the serene and apparently immutable complacency of my Edwardian youth, I must endeavour to revive the sugary notes of those far-off melodies floating across the chasm of so many years: 'O Sole Mio', perhaps, or 'La Petite Tonkinoise'—sentimental and tinkling, as we used to hear them performed on a fine spring day in Teviot Street by the gay, brittle strumming of a barrel-organ.

L' Envoi

As soon as I could write, I learnt to inscribe my address on the fly-leaves of books—an act which I believed sincerely was sufficient in itself to make them mine—and at the top of letter-paper. As children do, I spun it out as lengthily and as comprehensively as possible:

St Michael's Vicarage,
St Leonard's Road,
Bromley-by-Bow,
Poplar,
London,
England,
Europe,
The Western Hemisphere,
The World.

That was where I lived, and very proud of it I was, too; and proud of living in one of the more notorious slums: a similar arrogance to that displayed by people who endured the worst war-bombing. I felt real compassion for those who did not inhabit the largest city in the world; and how pitiable, when asked where you were born, not to be able to say: 'London!'

It had never occurred to me that we could ever live anywhere else, and when in the summer of 1913—last complete year of Edwardian security—I was told by my parents that we were moving to the country, and by Nanny that she was obliged to leave us, I felt as though the solid pavements were crumbling beneath my feet, that I was sliding towards the very brink of a precipice.

Over the prospect of Nanny's departure I was inconsolable; and my parents wisely made no attempt to offer any specious comfort. As to leaving Poplar, I listened with extreme prejudice to the various compensatory advantages put forward by my mother. There would be country air and walks; I should be able to have a *real* garden and lots of other children to play with; Scamp and Jack would have a much happier existence.

I wanted none of these things. I was content by now with my own company alleviated by Nanny's constant attendance and occasionally by the society of Maggie; and my patch of sterile soil suited me well enough. I wanted only the *status quo:* the view from my nursery, Chrisp Street Market, Stink Bridge and the bustle of the East India Dock Road. No country ramble could ever provide the rewards and interests of my peregrinations round the Docks. Those future benefits struck me as meretricious; and by a sort of instinct I divined that my parents also felt them to be scarcely worth the abandoning of that church and parish they had grown to love so well.

The crux of the matter, of course, was my father's tendency to recurring ill-health. He had filled his church and set the whole parochial machinery running smooth as well-oiled clockwork; common sense dictated that he should bid farewell to those stalwarts who were Christians for seven days of the week—or not at all; that my mother should take her leave of those women and children who needed her help so desperately. As for myself, I was ten years old; high time that I should be taken away from the dirt and the smells, the Chinamen and the dockers with their lusty oaths, the gin-sodden women hanging round the pubs; high time that I should learn to frequent polite children's parties instead of the Tunnel Gardens, to watch village sports in lieu of drunken squabbles.

Memory is even more unpredictable than the weather. It can preserve a tone of voice, a scent, a tint; but for some extraordinary reason—possibly not unconnected with mercifulness—I have not the slightest recollection of saying good-bye to Nanny nor of leaving Poplar. Not the slightest. That moment when Nanny and I had to part has been lost in a perpetual oblivion; like the moment when I walked out of the Vicarage for the last time, it has vanished from my consciousness.

Yet it must have happened; that high, green-painted gate that I could never open must have closed finally behind me. Useless now to prop it ajar with a stone, or wait for the policeman on the beat to lean over and unlatch it; I no longer had the right to do so.

At some moment of time—strangely veiled by an impenetrable curtain of forgetfulness—I must have turned my back on it for ever and faced, with apprehension and yet with curiosity, whatever lay ahead.